Monitor Comprehension

WEEK 1 DAY 1

READ THE PASSAGE Think about what is happening in this scene.

The Big Interview

Charles sat in the cafeteria with five other students, waiting for Ms. Swanson to interview all of them. Ms. Swanson, the seventh-grade science teacher, was looking for a lab helper. Charles's palms were sweaty and his face felt hot. He wondered if his face was red—and if anyone would notice.

As he prepared for his interview, Charles reviewed a set of index cards with notes that he had made earlier. On each card, he had written an answer to a question that Ms. Swanson might ask. "The emergency eyewash station is not a place to get a drink of water," he quietly read aloud from one card.

Charles decided to check out the other candidates. Nearby, a girl with dark red hair was shuffling her own set of index cards. He watched as she tore a card into tiny pieces and stuffed the pieces into a pocket. Suddenly she looked up at Charles. "Are you nervous?" she asked.

"No, I'm not nervous—not at all," Charles stammered. "What about you?"

"Uh, no, me neither," the girl responded.

At that moment, Ms. Swanson appeared. "Charles Locke?" she called out.

STRATEGY PRACTICE Look back at the passage. Underline the sentences and phrases that tell you Charles is nervous.

SKILL PRACTICE Read the item. Write your response.

1. What is this text about?

   _____

   _____

2. Is the girl nervous? Use text evidence in your response.

   _____

   _____

3. What is likely to happen next?

   _____

   _____

© Evan-Moor Corp. • EMC 6365 • Daily Reading Comprehension

Monitor Comprehension — WEEK 1 DAY 2

READ THE PASSAGE Read slowly. Think about the main idea of each section.

In a Pickle

With the right supplies, you can make your own pickles at home.

A Clean Start

All supplies that you use must be very clean when you make pickles at home. A dirty jar or spoon can spoil an entire batch of pickles.

The Cucumber Is King

The perfect pickle is crunchy. It starts with a firm, fresh cucumber. To make fresh pickles, fill jars with freshly picked cucumbers. Then pour a heated mixture of salt, vinegar, and spices into the jars. Seal the jars with clean lids. Allow the pickles to cool, and put the jars in the refrigerator. Write the date on the jars.

Timing Is Everything

Leave your homemade pickles in the refrigerator. Pay attention to the date on the jars. If you haven't eaten the pickles after six months, throw them away.

Other Pickled Foods

In addition to making pickles at home, you can try pickling other vegetables. Pickled carrots, cauliflower, and garlic cloves make tasty snacks and give salads some extra flavor.

STRATEGY PRACTICE Explain to a partner how using the section headings helped you understand the text.

SKILL PRACTICE Read the item. Write your response.

1. Under which heading did the author list the ingredients necessary for making pickles?

2. Is this text a recipe for making pickles? How can you tell?

3. What is the final step in making pickles?

Monitor Comprehension — WEEK 1 DAY 3

READ THE INTERVIEW Pause after reading each of the interviewer's questions. Think about the question as you read Sadie's answer.

Sadie Caddock, Animator

Interviewer: What is the best part about your job as an animator?

Sadie Caddock: I love getting a chance to bring a character to life. If I can imagine it, I can make it happen on the screen. It's a great feeling.

Interviewer: What was your favorite project?

Sadie Caddock: My favorite project was a movie called *It's a Zoo Out There*. Unlike commercials and TV shows, a full-length movie lets you explore the characters and story. I worked with a fun team of animators to create more than thirty animal characters.

Interviewer: How long does it take you to finish a project?

Sadie Caddock: It depends. A short commercial might take me a week to finish my part of it. The movie took more than a year. It also depends on whether I'm drawing by hand or using a computer. Computers make the work go much faster. However, I sometimes find that drawing by hand is more creative.

STRATEGY PRACTICE Did you understand all of Sadie Caddock's answers? Which answer would you like to know more about? Explain why.

_____

_____

SKILL PRACTICE Read the item. Write your response.

1. What is this kind of text called? How do you know?

_____

_____

2. What is the purpose of the boldfaced words in the text?

_____

_____

3. What is Sadie Caddock's favorite part of her job? Use text evidence in your response.

_____

Monitor Comprehension — WEEK 1, DAY 4

READ THE INFORMATION Think about how the information in this book is organized.

Contents

Introduction 5

Chapter 1: History of Pancakes 8

Chapter 2: Pancake Recipes 27

Chapter 3: Syrups and Toppings 40

Chapter 4: Pancake Contests 64

Chapter 5: Flapjack Fables 98

How It All Began

Pancakes are one of the oldest foods. The ancient Romans ate a mixture of milk, flour, eggs, and spices called *alita dolcia*.

Pancakes were special in medieval Europe. That's when the tradition of Pancake Day began. Pancake Day is the last day before Lent, a period of 40 days before Easter. On this day, people made pancakes to use up all of their eggs and butter, which were forbidden during Lent. Around the 1600s, writer William Shakespeare mentioned pancakes in two of his plays. These cakes go back a long way!

STRATEGY PRACTICE Based on the table of contents, what are two specific things that you might learn about pancakes by reading this book? Explain.

_____
_____

SKILL PRACTICE Read the item. Write your response.

1. Write the main idea of "How It All Began" in your own words. On which page would this text probably appear?

_____
_____

2. You want information about an event in which runners toss a pancake in a frying pan. Which chapter would you look in and why?

_____
_____

3. Bryant wonders how to make chocolate chip pancakes. What is the name of the chapter he should look in?

_____

Monitor Comprehension — WEEK 1, DAY 5

READ THE PASSAGE As you read, think about how Jamie feels.

A Long Day

Jamie was tired. She had been on her feet for hours. Her mom owned a small but busy restaurant in town. Three of her mom's employees had called in sick that morning. There was a big festival in the city park that day, and Jamie had wanted to go. But her mom had asked for her help at the restaurant.

All Jamie wanted to do was sit down for a while. Instead, she hurried around the restaurant, taking orders and refilling coffee cups. As soon as one table was cleared, a new set of customers walked in. The customers just kept coming! That meant more orders and more coffee.

"Order up!" called the cook from the kitchen. Jamie stared at the kitchen. She thought about all of the food stalls at the festival. Cooks there were preparing special foods from all over the world. Jamie imagined the delicious smells of new and exotic foods.

"Hurry, Jamie!" the cook called, catching Jamie lost in thought.

"I'm coming," Jamie grumbled. But her mom had already picked up the plates of hot food from the counter and delivered them to a table by the window.

"Wake up, Jamie," her mom said. "I know you don't want to be here, but I need your help."

STRATEGY PRACTICE Describe how you think Jamie feels and why she feels that way.

_____

_____

SKILL PRACTICE Read the item. Write your response.

1. Why is Jamie daydreaming?

_____

_____

2. What event caused Jamie's mother to need help?

_____

_____

3. What will Jamie probably do when she leaves the restaurant?

_____

_____

Make Connections — WEEK 2, DAY 1

READ THE PASSAGE As you read about the Snowdonia hawkweed, think of other rare plants and animals you know of, and think about how people treat rare things.

Rare and Beautiful Blooms

One of the rarest flowering plants in the world, the Snowdonia hawkweed, grows wild only in Snowdonia National Park in northern Wales. The region is rocky and mountainous, and the air is cool and damp. The Snowdonia hawkweed prefers this habitat. In fact, it grows nowhere else in the world. It is even picky about where it grows in the park.

Snowdonia hawkweed is about 11 inches (28 cm) tall. Its bright yellow blossoms have thin petals with ragged edges. The Snowdonia hawkweed may not be the most beautiful plant in the world, but it is a favorite snack of sheep.

In 1953, the Snowdonia hawkweed disappeared. People feared that the plant was gone forever. They believed that sheep grazing on the land had eaten the last few plants. So, the people who ran the park removed the sheep from the area, hoping that the hawkweed might return. Forty-nine years later, a group of plant scientists found the yellow flowers blooming in one spot in the park. The hawkweed had returned!

Scientists collected seeds from the plant in case it disappeared again. But since 2002, the rare plant has continued to bloom in the park.

STRATEGY PRACTICE Describe something rare or special that you have seen and where you saw it.

_____

_____

SKILL PRACTICE Read the item. Write your response.

1. Describe the climate in Snowdonia National Park.

_____

_____

2. Will Snowdonia hawkweed become common? Explain.

_____

_____

3. How did the plant scientists feel when they discovered Snowdonia hawkweed in 2002?

_____

_____

Make Connections — WEEK 2, DAY 2

READ THE PASSAGE — Think about how Jacob and his mom probably feel.

The Greatest Trick

Jacob burst into the kitchen holding a deck of cards. "The great Jacob performs his most amazing trick yet!" he shouted.

His little sister cooed and giggled from her highchair, but Jacob's mom was less amused. "Could you show me in a minute?" she pleaded. "I'm trying to feed Emma."

"It'll be quick," Jacob responded. "Pick a card, any card!" he called out, spreading the cards into a fan shape. His mother sighed and pointed at a card. Jacob plucked the card from the fanned deck and stuck it onto his forehead. "I cannot see your card with my eyes," he said, tapping his forehead with his finger, "but my mind's eye will reveal it to me. It's the ace of clubs!"

Emma laughed and opened her eyes wide. "Cubs!" she said, clapping her hands.

Jacob's mom looked at the baby and laughed. Jacob peeled the card off his forehead and shook Emma's tiny hand. "My new assistant," he said.

STRATEGY PRACTICE — Describe a personal experience that the passage reminded you of.

_____
_____
_____

SKILL PRACTICE — Read the item. Write your response.

1. What is the setting of this story?

_____
_____

2. Why did the author write this text?

_____
_____

3. Does Jacob's mom appreciate his magic trick? Explain.

_____
_____
_____

Make Connections — **WEEK 2, DAY 3**

READ THE PASSAGE As you read about the Rockettes, think about other activities that require a lot of skill and practice.

The Famous Rockettes

Imagine a long line of dancers performing a difficult high kick at exactly the same time. That was the vision of Russell Markert, who came up with the idea for the Rockettes back in 1925. The Rockettes, an all-female dance group, have come a long way with their high kicks. They have performed at the Radio City Music Hall in New York City since its opening in 1932.

The goal of the Rockettes is for all of the dancers to make the same movements at the exact same time, as if they were one person rather than 36. This task requires a lot of practice, skill, and cooperation. The Rockettes perform in more than 200 shows over a two-month period. The schedule requires a huge commitment from the dancers.

Over the years, more than 3,000 women have danced as Rockettes. They say that performing with the group is a dream come true, despite the long hours of practice and the demanding schedule. They love it when the audience stands and cheers.

STRATEGY PRACTICE Write about a time when you saw an athlete or performer do something amazing. How did remembering that event help you understand the passage?

_____
_____
_____

SKILL PRACTICE Read the item. Write your response.

1. For what two skills are the Rockettes best known?

_____
_____

2. What is Russell Markert's relationship to the Rockettes?

_____
_____

3. Do the Rockettes tend to enjoy their jobs? Use text evidence in your response.

_____
_____

Make Connections — WEEK 2, DAY 4

READ THE PASSAGE As you read about Juliana Chen, think about other successful people you have met or read about.

World Champion Magician

As a young girl growing up in China, Juliana Chen never imagined the success she would have as a performer. At just 10 years old, she was chosen to attend the Hunan Academy for the Performing Arts. The Hunan Academy is one of China's best schools for dancers, acrobats, and other kinds of performers.

Juliana first trained in ballet. Then she studied juggling and acrobatics and joined a famous acrobatic troupe. But the work was physically difficult, and Juliana injured her leg several times. While she was recovering from one of her injuries, Juliana watched a magic show on television. That's when Juliana knew she would become a magician.

Juliana impressed people with her special skill. Because of her acrobatic training, she was skilled with her body and her hands. She could make cards appear out of thin air, it seemed. In 1986, Juliana won the All-China Best Magician competition.

After her success in China, Juliana immigrated to Canada. There, she became an even bigger star. Soon, she traveled around the world, learning new tricks and performing in front of royalty. In 1997, she became the first woman and the first magician from China to win a world title for a solo act at the World Congress of Magicians, a major competition for magicians. Juliana continues to teach, perform, win awards, and learn new magic tricks.

STRATEGY PRACTICE What qualities help some people, including Juliana Chen, become successful?

_____

_____

SKILL PRACTICE Read the item. Write your response.

1. How do ballet, juggling, and acrobatics require similar skills?

_____

_____

2. Name two adjectives that describe Juliana. Explain your choices.

_____

_____

3. "She became the first woman and the first magician from China to win a world title for a solo act at the World Congress of Magicians." What conclusion can you draw about magicians based on this statement?

_____

Make Connections — WEEK 2, DAY 5

READ THE PASSAGE Think about how Kelly and Alicia feel about their summer plans.

Gardens and Grades

On most Sunday afternoons, Kelly and Alicia met in the treehouse of the big elm tree that grew between their backyards. Alicia brought a blanket to sit on, and Kelly brought snacks. On this warm June day, the girls looked down onto the lawns and driveways in their neighborhood. Usually they had trouble not talking at the same time. Today, neither said much.

"Thanks for the snack," Alicia said after a while. She was thinking about the next day. Her father had agreed to increase her allowance if she took care of the garden all summer. She wanted to earn enough money to pay for guitar lessons. But the garden was very big.

"You're welcome," answered Kelly. She was thinking about summer school, which she would begin the next day. Kelly wanted to improve her math skills so she would have an easier time in sixth grade.

The two girls sat glumly in their treehouse, thinking about the work ahead of them. "I wish we could trade places," they both said suddenly. They looked at each other and began to laugh.

STRATEGY PRACTICE Describe a time when you worked hard for something you wanted.

_____
_____
_____

SKILL PRACTICE Read the item. Write your response.

1. What is the reason that both girls are quiet?

_____
_____

2. Why do the girls wish they could trade places?

_____
_____

3. Are Kelly and Alicia sisters? How can you tell?

_____
_____

Visualization — WEEK 3, DAY 1

READ THE PASSAGE — Read slowly and notice details about how the flowers look, smell, and taste.

Flowers for Dinner

Flowers might look pretty on the dinner table. But what about serving them for dinner? In many cultures all around the world, people eat and enjoy different flowers in a variety of dishes.

The purple flowers of the lavender plant add a sweet lemon taste to chocolate cake or ice cream. Pansies, which have a grassy flavor, are a delicious addition to green salads. Bright yellow dandelion petals look cheerful when sprinkled over rice. Squash blossoms can be fried or stuffed with cheese. And the flowers of plants such as jasmine and chamomile are commonly used to make tea.

Does snacking on flowers sound weird? You may have eaten flowers already without realizing it! Several vegetables, such as cauliflower and broccoli, are actually flower buds. Broccoli forms tiny yellow blossoms as it continues to grow. Artichokes, if left on their stalks, form fuzzy purple blooms. And asparagus tips open into small pale green or white flowers.

If you're interested in eating flowers, be sure to learn about the plants first. Not every flower is safe to eat. The best way to find a tasty—and safe—flower is to visit your local grocery store.

STRATEGY PRACTICE — Draw a picture to show how you visualized one of the flowers that can be eaten.

SKILL PRACTICE — Read the item. Write your response.

1. How are broccoli and lavender similar?

2. What should you learn before eating a plant's flowers?

3. What is the main idea of the third paragraph?

Visualization — WEEK 3, DAY 2

READ THE PASSAGE Look for details that help you visualize each competition described in the passage.

Crazy Contests

When you think about competitions, you probably think of sports such as basketball and football. Not all serious competitive events are athletic, though. One example is the Rock Paper Scissors World Championship, in which contestants compete for large cash prizes.

Rock Paper Scissors is a simple game between two players. Each player counts to three and then "throws" one hand forward, making one of three hand signals. A fist means "rock," a flat hand means "paper," and two extended fingers in a V shape means "scissors." Rock wins against scissors, scissors wins against paper, and paper wins against rock. Although the game is simple, many players claim that they have developed complex strategies for winning.

Some people might consider a Rock Paper Scissors contest to be strange. Around the world, though, people compete in many events that others think are crazy. In England, a 200-year-old competition sends hundreds of people running down a hill, chasing a giant wheel of cheese. In Finland, hopeful guitar heroes compete in the Air Guitar World Championships by strumming invisible guitars in front of an audience. Wales hosts the yearly World Bog Snorkeling Championships, in which contestants wear silly costumes—dressed, for example, like a mermaid or an octopus—and swim through dark, stinky bog water as the crowd cheers.

These competitions are just a few of the crazy games that people play around the world. With some practice and training, maybe you could be a prize-winner in one of those contests yourself!

STRATEGY PRACTICE Which competition was easiest for you to visualize? Why?

_____

_____

SKILL PRACTICE Read the item. Write your response.

1. What is probably the runners' goal in the English competition mentioned in this text?

_____

_____

2. Would you enjoy playing Rock Paper Scissors? Explain.

_____

_____

3. How are the contestants probably judged in the Air Guitar World Championships?

_____

_____

Visualization WEEK 3 DAY 3

READ THE PASSAGE Look for words and phrases that help you visualize cockroaches.

Cockroach Fun Facts

When you think of interesting animals, you probably don't picture the common cockroach. However, although this insect isn't very pretty, it is pretty amazing.

Cockroaches are good at getting around. They can squeeze into very tight spaces, which comes in handy when they want to go through cracks in walls. A baby cockroach can flatten itself as thin as a dime. They're fast-moving bugs, too. Traveling at 3 miles an hour (4.8 km/h), a cockroach can easily scurry out of the way of looming feet or bug swatters.

Cockroaches are also tough. They can survive a month without food and a week without water. They can even survive for weeks without a head!

Next time you see a cockroach, show some respect for this common household pest. After all, the species has been around far longer than people—more than 280 million years, by some estimates. Now that's an old bug!

STRATEGY PRACTICE List at least two traits of cockroaches. For each trait, draw a picture that shows what you visualized.

SKILL PRACTICE Read the item. Write your response.

1. Why did the author compare a baby cockroach to a dime?

2. What is the most surprising fact in this text? Use text evidence in your response.

3. Picture a cockroach on your bathroom floor. You try to step on it, but it scuttles away. Where does it go?

Visualization — WEEK 3, DAY 4

READ THE PASSAGE Look for details that help you form a mental image of the animal shelter.

A Sheltered Life

If you visit the animal shelter in Salinas, California, you'll see giant wood cutouts of a dog and a cat. These signs were placed in front of the building to catch people's attention. The supersized cutouts make people curious and encourage them to visit the shelter—and maybe even adopt a pet. Each year, the Salinas shelter takes in around 2,000 dogs and 2,000 cats. The animals are either strays or are dropped off by people who couldn't take care of them. Of the 4,000 animals, some of them are eventually adopted into new homes. Some animals are transferred to other shelters. And, unfortunately, some cannot be saved because they are too sick or are considered dangerous.

Animal shelters provide food, medicine, and a safe place for animals to sleep. But they are not ideal homes. The shelters are loud, and the animals stay in small cages. The people who work at shelters do their best to care for the animals, but the animals do not always get the attention or exercise they need.

To prevent so many animals from becoming homeless, pet owners should take good care of their pets. One of the best ways to care for pets is to spay or neuter them. This surgery prevents cats and dogs from having more babies. And that reduces the number of homeless animals that end up in shelters.

STRATEGY PRACTICE Describe how you pictured the animal shelter in Salinas.

_____

_____

SKILL PRACTICE Read the item. Write your response.

1. What is the main idea of this text?

_____

_____

2. What can a good home offer a pet that an animal shelter cannot?

_____

_____

3. What is the author's opinion on spaying and neutering? How can you tell?

_____

_____

Visualization — WEEK 3, DAY 5

READ THE PASSAGE As you read, picture the setting and the characters in the story.

Getting the Perfect Shot

The Cardona family was growing restless. Mr. and Mrs. Cardona had wanted a simple photo taken for their family's summer newsletter. Ms. Rourke, the photographer, was looking through her camera but wasn't taking any pictures.

"There isn't enough light on Mr. Cardona's moustache," she said to Jamila, her assistant. Jamila sighed, moved the lamp an inch to the left, and glanced at the family. The couple's two sons were starting to fidget. Jamila knew that they would soon start to complain. It was time to take the picture.

"Now Mrs. Cardona's hair looks too frizzy," Ms. Rourke remarked. "Jamila, please get the styling products." When Jamila returned, she noticed that the boys were giggling and poking each other. Their parents' smiles were drooping under the hot lights.

"Oh, now the boys are standing at the wrong angle," Ms. Rourke announced.

Mr. Cardona's face turned red. His wife looked like she was about to cry. Jamila quickly stepped up to the camera and snapped the picture. "All done!" she said. Everyone looked relieved, except for Ms. Rourke.

STRATEGY PRACTICE Choose a character from the story. Describe what the character looks like.

_____

_____

SKILL PRACTICE Read the item. Write your response.

1. What is the setting of this text? How can you tell?

_____

_____

2. What do Jamila and the Cardonas have in common?

_____

_____

3. What will Ms. Rourke probably do now?

_____

_____

Organization — WEEK 4 DAY 1

READ THE PASSAGE Think about how the different kinds of salt are similar and different.

Flavoring the Globe

Most people are familiar with plain white table salt. But if you think that salt is just a bunch of tiny white crystals, you're mistaken. This common seasoning has many different colors and flavors.

French sea salt comes from seawater. The larger grains and milder flavor of this salt make it a popular choice for meals. Some people even like to sprinkle it on chocolate cakes and cookies.

Hawaiian sea salt, on the other hand, has a rosy color that comes from the clay in the region. The mellow flavor of the salt is perfect for pork dishes.

Like Hawaiian sea salt, Australian river salt is also pink. Its color, however, comes from algae in the groundwater. The soft pink flakes melt easily on warm foods.

Mediterranean black lava salt resembles tiny cubes of coal. This salt is made by mixing sea salt from the Mediterranean Sea with charcoal from volcanic lava. The dark crystals, unlike the other salts mentioned, add a dramatic color contrast to baked potatoes.

Sampling different salts is a wonderful way to travel the world without leaving home! Try sprinkling one of the many varieties of salt on your food and enjoy the unique flavor and texture.

STRATEGY PRACTICE How are the different kinds of salt mentioned in the passage similar? How are they different?

_____
_____
_____

SKILL PRACTICE Read the item. Write your response.

1. How are Hawaiian and Australian salts alike?

_____
_____

2. Which salt in the text has an added ingredient? What is the ingredient?

_____
_____

3. How does the author guide the reader from familiar salt to exotic salts?

_____
_____

Organization — WEEK 4, DAY 2

READ THE PASSAGE Pay attention to how the main idea and details about synchronized swimming are organized.

A Splashy Sport

The sport of synchronized swimming is one part swimming, one part dancing, and one part gymnastics. This unique sport features a pair or a team of athletes performing acrobatic routines in the water. It is one of the most difficult sports because it requires concentration, athletic skill, endurance, and gracefulness.

Professional synchronized swimmers need strong basic skills. They must be good swimmers and must be able to hold their breath underwater for long periods of time. They must also be able to tread water, supporting themselves without touching the bottom of the pool. The swimmers learn challenging moves, such as holding themselves upside down vertically in the water while moving their legs and rotating their bodies. They also learn how to lift their teammates out of the water and to stay perfectly in sync with each other.

You will find synchronized swim teams throughout the country. They compete with each other and give performances to audiences of all ages. The sport of synchronized swimming is sure to take your breath away, whether you're watching or participating.

STRATEGY PRACTICE What details does the author use in the second paragraph to support the main idea expressed in the first paragraph? List at least two details.

_____

_____

SKILL PRACTICE Read the item. Write your response.

1. Describe the purpose of each paragraph in this text.

_____

_____

2. In the second paragraph, why does the author include a definition for the phrase "tread water"?

_____

_____

3. How many sentences in the last paragraph are facts? How can you tell?

_____

_____

© Evan-Moor Corp. • EMC 6365 • Daily Reading Comprehension

WEEK 4
Organization
DAY 3

READ THE PASSAGE Look for cause-and-effect relationships and how the author uses them to organize the text.

Dandelions to the Rescue

Some people consider the hardy dandelion to be an annoying weed, despite its sunny yellow blossoms, because it grows quickly and chokes out other plants. These people work hard, therefore, to remove dandelions from their lawns. However, this useful plant has played an important role in American history. And it may even have found its way to your dinner table.

Early settlers brought the dandelion from Europe to North America, and, as a result, the aggressive plant spread. But the settlers had a good reason for bringing the plant with them. They relied on dandelions for food and medicine. They ate the green leaves and roasted the roots to make a hot drink. Because dandelion greens are a good source of vitamins and minerals, it is likely that dandelions saved lives during times when food was scarce.

You don't have to be a starving settler to eat tasty dandelion greens. The key is to pick the leaves in the spring, before the flowers form. The young leaves are tender and less bitter. You can add the smaller leaves to salads, but larger leaves should be steamed to bring out the flavor. Put a little salt and olive oil on the greens. You'll be surprised by how tasty this common weed can be.

STRATEGY PRACTICE Underline the words and phrases that signal a cause-and-effect relationship. Then describe one effect of eating dandelions.

_____

_____

SKILL PRACTICE Read the item. Write your response.

1. How did dandelions save the lives of early American settlers?

_____

_____

2. Why do so many people fight against dandelions despite their good qualities?

_____

_____

3. Are there any opinions in the third paragraph? Explain.

_____

_____

Week 4 • Organization • Day 4

READ THE PASSAGE Think about how the events in the passage are organized.

A Tasty Accident

Antonio López de Santa Anna, a former president of Mexico, was living in New York in the late 1860s. While he was there, he met with Thomas Adams, an inventor. Santa Anna shared with Adams his idea for an invention—a new process, really, for making rubber products such as tires.

Rubber is a natural product, but it's expensive. Santa Anna thought it would be possible to blend the rubber with chicle (CHIK-ul), the milky juice of a tropical tree. That would make rubber products much cheaper to produce. Adams told Santa Anna that he was willing to try. Later, Santa Anna arranged for one ton of chicle to be shipped to Adams from Mexico.

Adams experimented for about a year, trying different blends of rubber and chicle. None of them were successful. The inventor still had plenty of chicle left over and wondered what to do with it. Then he remembered Santa Anna's stories of people chewing chicle in Mexico. So Adams made a small batch of chewing gum, packaged it, and sold it in local stores. The soft and springy gum was much tastier than other American gum, which was made from wax or tree sap.

Although Adams's original idea was a failure, chewing gum was a success. In 1871, he invented a machine to manufacture gum so he wouldn't have to make it by hand. Adams enjoyed success for the rest of his life, and people have enjoyed all kinds of tasty gum for years.

STRATEGY PRACTICE Underline the words, phrases, and dates that signal sequence. Then summarize what Adams did with the leftover chicle.

_____

_____

SKILL PRACTICE Read the item. Write your response.

1. Write the main idea of this text in your own words.

_____

_____

2. Are there any opinions in the first paragraph? How can you tell?

_____

_____

3. Explain the purpose of each paragraph in the text.

_____

_____

Organization — WEEK 4, DAY 5

READ THE PASSAGE — Think about the sequence that the author uses to tell the events of the story.

The Rafting Trip

Tina took the helmet from Dale, the rafting instructor who would be guiding the group down the river. Tina pushed her hair out of her face and fitted the helmet on her head. Then she fastened the strap. "I've never had to wear a helmet on a boat before," she complained.

"This isn't really a boat," said Dale. "It's a raft," he explained in a casual tone. "A raft is filled with air and it doesn't have an engine." Dale picked up a stack of life jackets and began distributing them to people as they waited to climb into the raft. "We'll hit some choppy water in the river," he told everyone. "And we want all of you to be safe."

"But I feel silly in this helmet," Tina said. "Do I really need it?" Stepping forward to get a life jacket, she caught her foot in a rope that was coiled up near the raft. Tina stumbled forward in surprise and, with a shriek, fell down onto the pile of rope.

Dale smiled at Tina as she untangled herself. "Yes, you really do need it," he answered, holding out his hand to help Tina up.

Tina stood up carefully. "You know," she said, "I think you're right."

STRATEGY PRACTICE — What is the message of the story, and which paragraph delivers the message?

_____
_____
_____

SKILL PRACTICE — Read the item. Write your response.

1. Why did the author probably use dialogue to tell this story?

_____
_____

2. Why did Dale insist that everyone wear a helmet?

_____
_____

3. What causes Tina to change her attitude about helmet use?

_____
_____

Determine Important Information — WEEK 5, DAY 1

READ THE INTERVIEW Think about the information that the interviewer is trying to learn from Janette Flores.

Planning a Beautiful Day

Janette Flores is a wedding planner in Baltimore, Maryland. **Bubbly Bride** magazine wanted to find out what it takes for a professional to plan one of the most important days of someone's life.

Bubbly Bride: What happens in a typical day for a wedding planner?

Janette Flores: Planning a wedding involves much more than the wedding day itself. I start at least six months in advance, calling catering companies and arranging flower deliveries and dress fittings.

Bubbly Bride: What do you do on the day of the wedding?

Janette Flores: I make sure everything goes smoothly. No matter how carefully you plan, there can often be last-minute problems or surprises.

Bubbly Bride: Have you planned any weddings that you think are especially memorable?

Janette Flores: Every wedding I plan is memorable for a different reason. One couple, both scuba divers, wanted to get married under water. Another couple wanted to exchange vows on the train where they had met. The best weddings reflect the couple's personalities.

STRATEGY PRACTICE Summarize the tasks that Janette Flores does in her job.

_____

_____

SKILL PRACTICE Read the item. Write your response.

1. What is the purpose of the paragraph before the first question?

_____

_____

2. Who is the primary audience for this kind of article? Explain.

_____

_____

3. Why did the author probably choose a question-and-answer format for this text?

_____

Determine Important Information — WEEK 5, DAY 2

READ THE PASSAGE Read the passage and study the chart.

Confidence

What is your *guerdon* (meaning "reward") for studying spelling? If you're Sameer Mishra, winner of the 2008 Scripps National Spelling Bee, knowing how to spell *guerdon* meant a reward of scholarships, cash prizes, and the title of the best speller in the United States.

The Scripps National Spelling Bee has challenged students since 1925. Students under the age of 15 train year-round for a chance to show their spelling skills to the world. Round 1 of the spelling bee is a written test. All other rounds are oral competitions. In the final rounds, spellers have one chance to spell a word correctly before elimination. It's an event that requires a lot of c-o-n-f-i-d-e-n-c-e.

Year	Winning Word	Champion
2001	succedaneum	Sean Conley
2002	prospicience	Pratyush Buddiga
2003	pococurante	Sai R. Gunturi
2004	autochthonous	David Scott Pilarski Tidmarsh
2005	appoggiatura	Anurag Kashyap
2006	Ursprache	Kerry Close
2007	serrefine	Evan M. O'Dorney
2008	guerdon	Sameer Mishra
2009	Laodicean	Kavya Shivashankar
2010	stromuhr	Anamika Veeramani

STRATEGY PRACTICE How might the chart be helpful to students who want to compete in the Scripps National Spelling Bee?

_____

_____

SKILL PRACTICE Read the item. Write your response.

1. How is the title related to the text?

_____

_____

2. Why does the last word in the text contain so many hyphens? Why did the author do this?

_____

_____

3. Which winners won by spelling proper nouns? How can you tell?

_____

_____

Determine Important Information — WEEK 5, DAY 3

READ THE INFORMATION Think about the information that these pages tell you about the book.

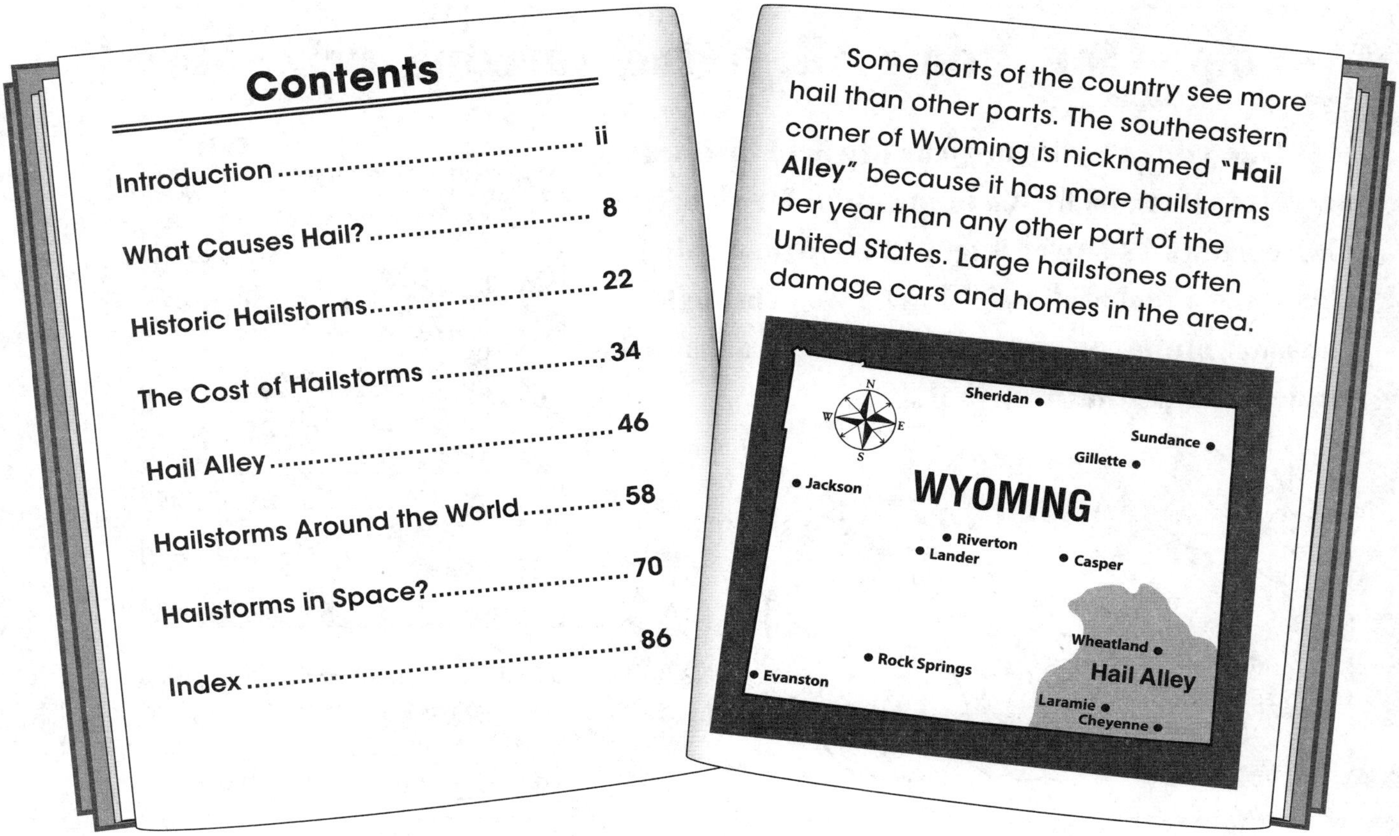

Contents

Introduction ii
What Causes Hail? 8
Historic Hailstorms 22
The Cost of Hailstorms 34
Hail Alley 46
Hailstorms Around the World 58
Hailstorms in Space? 70
Index 86

Some parts of the country see more hail than other parts. The southeastern corner of Wyoming is nicknamed "Hail Alley" because it has more hailstorms per year than any other part of the United States. Large hailstones often damage cars and homes in the area.

(Map of Wyoming showing Sheridan, Sundance, Gillette, Jackson, Riverton, Lander, Casper, Evanston, Rock Springs, Wheatland, Laramie, Cheyenne, with "Hail Alley" in the southeastern corner.)

STRATEGY PRACTICE In which section of the library would you most likely find this book? Explain.

_____
_____

SKILL PRACTICE Read the item. Write your response.

1. In which chapter would you find the page shown on the right? Explain.

_____
_____
_____

2. How would a reader most likely use the map?

_____
_____
_____

3. Describe the purpose of the part of the book that begins on page 86.

_____

Determine Important Information — WEEK 5 DAY 4

READ THE FLIER Think about how the information in the flier is arranged.

Come One, Come All, to the Amazing Maize Maze!

Make your way through a cornfield that has been transformed into a living maze for all ages. Our cornstalks tower 6 feet (2 m) high, making this maze a real challenge! Find a way through the maze alone, or use a whistle to call a trained guide to help you through it.

Admission: $5

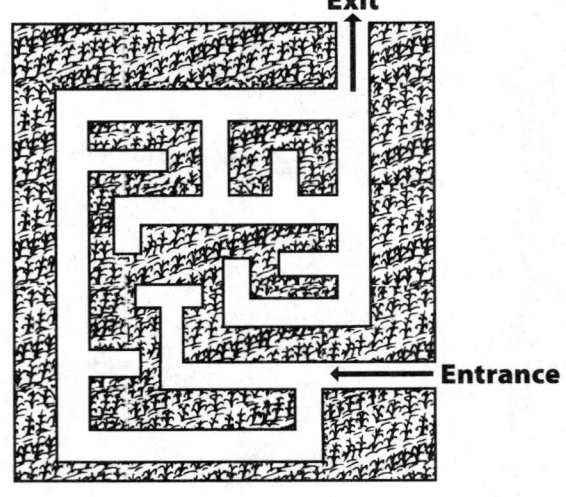

Directions to the **Amazing Maize Maze:** Take I–95 to Polk Road. Turn right onto Polk Road and drive 5.5 miles (9 km). Look for the signs after you pass McClintock Drive.

STRATEGY PRACTICE What information is important to know for people who are worried about getting lost in the maze? Why?

_____

SKILL PRACTICE Read the item. Write your response.

1. When should the driver start looking for the Amazing Maize Maze signs?

_____

2. What makes this maze so difficult?

_____

3. What information can be determined from the map of the maze?

_____

Determine Important Information

WEEK 5 DAY 5

READ THE INFORMATION Study the table of contents and read the excerpt.

Contents

Introduction	i
Dance Through the Centuries	3
Salsa	17
Belly Dancing	25
Hip-Hop	33
Tango	57
Ballet	71
Modern Dance	113

Breaking Away

From graceful ballroom dancing to rhythmic hip-hop, the modern world has had a big influence on the way we think about dance today.

In the early 1900s, American dancers began to turn against the traditions of ballet. The movements and costumes were too strict, they thought. Instead, they wanted to move more freely—to dance in their bare feet. They wanted to express emotions with their movement. That's how modern dance was born.

STRATEGY PRACTICE Which chapter would be most important for someone who wants to research the history of dance? Explain.

_____

_____

SKILL PRACTICE Read the item. Write your response.

1. In which chapter would you find the page shown on the right? How can you tell?

_____

_____

2. In which chapter would you look for information on how to become a ballerina? Explain.

_____

_____

3. What is the birthplace of modern dance? How do you know?

_____

_____

Ask Questions — WEEK 6, DAY 1

READ THE PASSAGE Think of a question to ask about Kobe beef. Look for the answer as you read.

The Rarest Beef

If you like hamburgers, you'd probably love a Kobe burger. Kobe beef comes from a rare type of cattle, called Wagyu. Technically, these cattle are raised only in the Kobe region of Japan. Kobe beef is prized for its flavor, tenderness, and delicate texture.

Wagyu cattle are raised on small farms in the lush green countryside of Japan, where farmland is scarce and, therefore, expensive. The cows have a special diet and are treated well. They even receive massages as a way to relax them and stimulate their muscles. Compared to typical cattle ranches, which tend to be crowded, Kobe farms are like paradise for the cattle.

As you might have guessed, Kobe beef is expensive. A Kobe steak can cost more than $100 per pound (0.45 kg). By comparison, most American-raised beef costs less than $10 per pound (0.45 kg).

Today, some U.S. ranchers raise Wagyu cattle crossed with Angus beef cattle. They call the meat Kobe-style beef, and many meat-lovers believe that the meat is quite tasty—even though the cows probably do not get massages.

STRATEGY PRACTICE Write a question you have about Kobe beef. Then write the answer if you found it.

_____
_____
_____

SKILL PRACTICE Read the item. Write your response.

1. What is the author's purpose for writing this text?

_____
_____

2. How does American-raised beef differ from Kobe beef?

_____
_____

3. Write two reasons why Kobe beef is ten times more expensive than U.S. beef.

_____
_____

Ask Questions

WEEK 6 DAY 2

READ THE PASSAGE Think of a question about Julius Erving. Look for the answer as you read.

An American Treasure

Floating, airborne, and *focused*—these words have often been used to describe how Julius "Dr. J" Erving played basketball. Erving became one of the best players in the sport. He forever changed the way people played basketball.

Erving started playing professional basketball in the 1970s. The sport was different then. It was mainly a floor game, with players running back and forth across the court. Unlike other players, Erving found that his skill was in the air, because he could leap far and high. He soon became known for his slam-dunks, which were not as common in the 1970s as they are today. Most players scored by throwing the ball toward the basket from far away. But Erving flew toward the board with the ball in hand, spinning his body in the air before sending the ball down through the hoop. This tremendous skill helped the teams he played for win three championships.

Dr. J says of his life, "I saw that basketball could be my way out, and I worked hard to make sure it was." This inspiring athlete discovered his unique skill early on and used it to his advantage throughout his life.

STRATEGY PRACTICE Write a question you have about Julius Erving. Then write the answer if you found it.

_____
_____
_____

SKILL PRACTICE Read the item. Write your response.

1. How did Erving differ from the other basketball players of the 1970s?

_____
_____

2. Why did the author probably choose this title?

_____
_____

3. How does the author feel about Julius Erving? Use text evidence in your response.

_____
_____

Ask Questions — WEEK 6, DAY 3

READ THE PASSAGE Stop after you read each paragraph and ask yourself a question about what you have read.

America's Littlest Big Eater

Think of the biggest meal you've ever eaten. It's likely that Sonya Thomas has eaten a lot more than that. The petite woman weighs only about 100 pounds (45 kg), yet she has smashed national and international records in competitive eating. Competitive eating events are contests to see who can eat the most of a certain kind of food in a set amount of time. When it comes to this competition, dainty diners need not apply.

Have you ever eaten lobster? Sonya can eat 44 of them in 12 minutes. How about french fries covered in chili and cheese? Sonya once ate more than 8 pounds (4 kg) of them in 10 minutes. Sonya has eaten 65 hard-boiled eggs in 6 minutes and 40 seconds. That's about half the time it takes to cook a single egg! You might eat a slice of cheesecake for dessert. Sonya once consumed 11 pounds (5 kg) of this rich dessert in just 9 minutes.

Sonya stays in shape by eating lots of fruits and vegetables and by avoiding junk food, except in competitions. She also exercises regularly. These habits not only help keep Sonya Thomas healthy but allow her to perform better in competitions.

STRATEGY PRACTICE Write a question that you thought of while reading. Write the answer if you found it.

_____

_____

SKILL PRACTICE Read the item. Write your response.

1. How are all eating competitions similar?

_____

_____

2. Why does the author mention Sonya's weight?

_____

_____

3. What is the author's purpose for including the facts in the second paragraph?

_____

_____

Ask Questions — WEEK 6, DAY 4

READ THE PASSAGE As you read, think of questions about the topic of shale oil.

Oil from a Stone

It may seem impossible to remove oil from a stone, but that hasn't stopped people from trying. Scientists argue that with new technology and creative thinking, getting oil from a stone may not be as difficult as we think. Of course, it also takes the right kind of rocks.

Shale oil is oil that exists in solid form within rock. This unique oil was formed from fossilized creatures from the Tertiary (TUR-shee-air-ee) period, about 65 million years ago, and high levels of heat and pressure.

Mining shale oil is much more difficult than removing liquid oil. Workers must take extra care to protect the surrounding area during this difficult procedure. Otherwise, the process can cause erosion and can pollute the groundwater. In addition, shale oil must be heated to extreme temperatures and must be refined even further after it has been pulled from the ground. The refining process, like the mining process, takes a lot of water. This is another serious concern.

Although it is hard to collect, shale oil has long-term potential. There is enough shale oil in the western United States to meet current oil demands for about 400 years. Some people say that with enough funding for research, shale oil could be collected easily one day.

STRATEGY PRACTICE Write a question that the passage answers. Then have a partner answer it.

_____
_____

SKILL PRACTICE Read the item. Write your response.

1. Write two reasons why retrieving shale oil is dangerous for the environment.

_____
_____

2. Cite the sentence in the text that lets you know the author's opinion of shale oil. Use quotation marks.

_____
_____

3. What is the purpose of the final paragraph?

_____
_____

Ask Questions
WEEK 6 DAY 5

READ THE PASSAGE Ask yourself questions to make sure you understand what you are reading.

The First Fish

David and his grandfather had been fishing all day. Right before the sun went down, David finally felt a fish take the bait. "Gotcha!" he called out, reeling in his line.

David's grandfather watched his grandson's struggle. He tipped open the cooler between them, where the eight fat fish he had caught earlier were placed on ice. "Easy now," he advised David. "You don't want to pull him in too fast."

Ignoring his grandfather, David jumped to his feet and turned the reel as fast as he could. "I can't let him get away! I've been waiting all day for this!"

Just when it seemed as if the fish would surface, David toppled backward onto the dock. The line had snapped, and it lay loosely coiled up across David's lap. His face fell. "There goes my first fish," he mumbled sadly.

His grandfather smiled knowingly. "It won't be your last," he said. "You'll bring in the next one."

STRATEGY PRACTICE Write a question you have about the story. Discuss it with a partner.

_____

_____

SKILL PRACTICE Read the item. Write your response.

1. What is the theme of this text?

_____

_____

2. Why is it effective to tell this story through dialogue?

_____

_____

3. How does David feel at the end of the story?

_____

_____

Main Idea and Details — WEEK 7, DAY 1

READ THE LETTER Read each paragraph of Melissa's letter. Decide what it is mostly about.

> Dear Johanna,
>
> How are you? My name is Melissa. I've been looking forward to having a pen pal for a long time now. I hope we can become great friends!
>
> Ever since I got your name and address from my teacher, Mrs. Sands, I have been thinking about what to write. First, I thought of giving you a description of what it's like to go to school here in Minnesota, but then I figured you could look up Minnesota on the Internet and read about it yourself. Then I had the idea to tell you about my family, but I realized that the story of my little brother losing a tooth or the time we got a new kitten might be kind of boring. After that, I thought about asking you questions about what it's like to live in Belgium, but I was afraid you might think my questions were silly.
>
> I guess I can tell you a little about myself. In fact, you've probably already learned one thing about me. I sometimes have a hard time making up my mind! I hope you will write me back anyway.
>
> Sincerely,
> Melissa

SKILL PRACTICE Read the item. Write your response.

1. How did Melissa get connected to Johanna?

___

2. Where does Johanna live? Cite text evidence in your answer.

___

3. How will Johanna probably feel when she receives Melissa's letter? Explain.

___

STRATEGY PRACTICE Write the main idea of the third paragraph in your own words.

___

Main Idea and Details — WEEK 7, DAY 2

READ THE PASSAGE Look for colorful details that tell about the topic of the passage.

Dog of the Millennium

You may have heard of dogs that can shake hands and roll over, but have you ever heard of a dog that knows more than 100 commands? For Endal, a yellow Labrador retriever, learning all those commands was just part of his job as a service dog. After naval officer Allen Parton suffered an injury in the Gulf War and was confined to a wheelchair, Endal came to live with Parton to help him recover from his injuries and resume a normal life.

Endal had to learn a lot in order to help his human partner. He learned to stand on his hind legs to pay for and collect a bus ticket. He even learned how to use a credit card at the grocery store! One time when Parton was struck by a car and thrown from his wheelchair, Endal covered him with a blanket, brought him a mobile phone, and alerted help. Endal's quick thinking and helpful response explains why Parton thought of the dog more as a partner than as a pet. It's no wonder that this wonder dog was named "Dog of the Millennium" by *Dogs Today* in 2002.

When Endal passed away at the age of 13, Parton felt sad but grateful. "He will be missed, but I really want to celebrate his life," Parton said.

SKILL PRACTICE Read the item. Write your response.

1. When and why did Endal go to live with Allen Parton?

2. Write three skills that Endal possessed that made him extraordinary.

3. Why was Endal named Dog of the Millenium? Was the title justified? Defend your stance.

STRATEGY PRACTICE What details describe what Endal did when Parton was hit by a car? Describe how you visualized the scene.

Sequence WEEK 7 DAY 3

READ THE PASSAGE Pay attention to the order of events for swimming with the Polar Bear Club.

The Coolest Club Around

Every Sunday from November through April, a group of men and women run shouting into the freezing waters of the Atlantic Ocean off the coast of New York City. Are they crazy? Maybe. Do they have a great time? Definitely.

The Coney Island Polar Bear Club was founded in 1903 by Bernarr Macfadden. He believed that a daily dip in cold water had big health benefits. He proclaimed this theory while in the freezing water as onlookers gawked. Today, men and women still flock to the Polar Bear Club's weekly outings as a way to "chill out." Water temperatures vary from about 60°F (16°C) down to about 33°F (0.6°C). Add to that the windchill factor, and you have one frosty swim!

Swimming with the Coney Island Polar Bear Club takes some preparation. First, you should check with your doctor before swimming in cold water to make sure you're in good physical health. Next, you'll need a bathing suit and a warm towel. Most members also wear special boots that protect their feet from rocks and other sharp objects on the beach. The boots also help keep their feet warm in the freezing water.

Once you're ready to go, it's just a matter of gathering the courage to make that big leap. Plenty of people end up at the water's edge and turn away at the last second. If you're sure you want the Polar Bear experience, you might want to bring a friend who won't let you leave until you've taken the plunge!

SKILL PRACTICE Read the item. Write your response.

1. Which sentence in the text tells what made Bernarr Macfadden run into the chilly Atlantic Ocean in 1903?

_____
_____

2. Why do the Polar Bear Club members wear special boots?

_____
_____

3. What should new Polar Bear members do before entering the chilly water?

_____

STRATEGY PRACTICE Underline the words and phrases in the passage that helped you understand what the people in the club do and why they do it.

Sequence — WEEK 7, DAY 4

READ THE PASSAGE Think about the sequence of events in Mira's visit to Hong Kong.

Mira's Visit

From the moment the airplane touched down at the Hong Kong airport, Mira knew she was in for an adventure. The busy airport was full of people bustling about. The people looked like they came from all over the world. Mira heard bits of conversation in many different languages.

Mira and her parents hurried to the hotel, where they checked in and dropped off their luggage. They were eager to begin exploring the city. Mira's dad brought a map and a detailed plan of what sights they would see.

The first stop on the list was the Hong Kong Wetland Park, just outside the city. The peaceful park had lots of places to walk, and Mira enjoyed sketching pictures of wildlife, including a crocodile lounging beside its private pool. On the train back to the city, the family marveled at the towering skyscrapers. Next, they stopped at the Science Museum, where Mira and her mom visited the World of Mirrors exhibit. After a lunch of local treats from a street-food cart, the family rushed to Victoria Harbor for the "Symphony of Lights." In the light show, beams of light were projected onto the buildings around the harbor and reflected off the calm waters below.

The family returned to the hotel, ready for a good night's sleep. Mira looked forward to another day of fun in Hong Kong. She was amazed to think of all they had done on their first day!

SKILL PRACTICE Read the item. Write your response.

1. About what time of day did Mira's plane land? How can you tell?

2. Between which two activities did the family eat supper?

3. Why did the author use the verbs "hurried" and "rushed"?

STRATEGY PRACTICE Choose one of the sites that Mira visited. Describe your mental image of it.

Main Idea and Details **WEEK 7**
Sequence **DAY 5**

READ THE PASSAGE Think about what Alex does and the order in which he does those things.

Hidden Treasure

When Alex first looked at the map, he thought it was just an old piece of newspaper. Looking closer, however, he noticed the instructions. He ran across the beach to show it to his older sister.

"Nina! Look at this!" he shouted, waving the map in her face. "What does it say?"

Nina stopped working on her sand castle and took the map from Alex's hands. "'Start at the dock and take three steps toward the water,'" she read aloud. "'Turn to the right and walk 20 steps. Dig 1 foot (30.5 cm) down for the key.' Alex, what is this?"

"It's a map for a hidden treasure!" Alex said breathlessly. He grabbed the map and struggled to sound out the words, reading slowly. "'Carry the key to the old boathouse.' Where's the boathouse, Nina?"

"It's over there," said Nina as she pointed toward the dock. "The instructions say to look for a yellow bird cage and then find a second key. Where did you get this map, Alex?"

Alex pointed toward a cluster of beach umbrellas. "Dad gave it to me," he said. Nina thought she could see their father pretending to read while he watched them talk, but he quickly ducked back behind his book. "He said a pirate gave it to him!" Alex exclaimed.

"I see," Nina said. She thought for a moment and then smiled brightly. "Well, let's go find some treasure."

SKILL PRACTICE Read the item. Write your response.

1. What is the third step in the treasure map's directions?

_____

_____

2. Which child is older? How can you tell?

_____

3. What does the map say to do once the children reach the boathouse?

_____

_____

STRATEGY PRACTICE Reread the last two paragraphs. Why does Nina say, "I see"? What does she realize?

_____

_____

WEEK 8 — Cause and Effect — DAY 1

READ THE PASSAGE — Think about the process of making paper and the result of each step.

Handmade Memories

Paper plays a major role in much of our lives, from books and magazines to birthday cards and notebook paper. For many people, making their own paper is a way of expressing their personalities. It is also a fun recycling project.

Making paper requires only a few special tools, including a blender and a small wire mesh screen. You can use computer paper, old cards, letters, and construction paper as your basic papermaking materials. If you want to make a darker paper, try using or adding newspaper. Materials such as colored string, rose petals, or even old bluejeans can add interesting tints and textures to your paper.

To start, tear or cut up the old paper you are using into small pieces. Add the cut pieces to warm water, and process the mixture in a blender until it is thick and soupy. Then add any other materials you want to use, such as bits of string. Next, spread the mixture on a screen. Using a cloth, press all the moisture out of the paper through the screen. Then carefully peel the damp paper away from the screen and let it dry for a few hours. When it has dried, you can use your paper in any way you choose.

Making your own paper allows you to add your special touch to an everyday material. Just think of all the people you could impress with your handmade paper gifts!

SKILL PRACTICE — Read the item. Write your response.

1. Why should you tear the paper into little pieces before putting it into the blender?

_____

_____

2. Why do you press on the soupy material on a screen?

_____

_____

3. You are making paper and add bits of orange-colored string to the mixture. How will that affect the final paper? Be specific.

_____

_____

STRATEGY PRACTICE — Write a brief summary of how to make paper, according to the passage.

_____

_____

Cause and Effect — WEEK 8, DAY 2

READ THE PASSAGE Think about why the pyramid was built and what is happening to it today.

A Pyramid in Wyoming

When you think of pyramids, you probably picture one in Egypt or Mexico. Did you know that there is also a pyramid in the United States? Not many people do. You can find the pyramid, called the Ames Monument, off a quiet dirt road in the southeast corner of Wyoming.

Back in the 1800s, two brothers named Oliver and Oakes Ames worked with the Union Pacific Railroad to build railroad tracks that stretched across the country. This was a spectacular feat. However, Oakes was later charged with dishonest business practices, so the Ames brothers and the railroad company gained a bad reputation. After the Ames brothers died, the people who ran Union Pacific wanted to restore the company's public image. So they built a monument near Sherman, a quiet town at the highest point along the rail line. The builder used blocks of pink granite found in the area to construct the monument—a 60-foot (18-meter) pyramid. An artist added two 9-foot-tall (3-meter-tall) carved portraits, one of each Ames brother.

At one time, train passengers traveling through the area could get off the train and view the pyramid up close. However, since then, the railroad tracks have been moved and the town of Sherman no longer exists. Few people come to see the Ames Monument anymore, and the odd structure has fallen into disrepair. As a result, this pyramid may eventually vanish into history.

SKILL PRACTICE Read the item. Write your response.

1. Why did the Union Pacific Railroad build the Ames Monument?

2. Write two reasons why the pyramid has fallen into disrepair.

3. Why might the monument "vanish into history"?

STRATEGY PRACTICE Write a question about the Ames Monument. Write the answer, too, if the passage provides that information.

Fact and Opinion — WEEK 8 DAY 3

READ THE PASSAGE Think about which details are facts and which express the author's opinions.

The World's Loneliest Phone Booth

For almost 40 years, a lone phone booth stood in the Mojave Desert about 75 miles (120 km) southwest of Las Vegas. It was likely installed for local miners around 1960. The glass panels were long gone from the booth by 1990, and the phonebook had been stolen. But a visitor to the booth in 1990 found that the telephone still worked. For the next 10 years, the world's loneliest phone booth became one of the oddest attractions in the world.

After its phone number was listed on the Internet, the phone in the Mohave booth began to ring more often. Visitors to the phone booth would often camp out, waiting for a chance to answer the special phone. Calls came in from many different states and even different countries. Visitors were thrilled to be able to answer the phone and talk to strangers from distant places. They were happy to share their own stories as they "reached across the miles."

In May 2000, Pacific Bell Telephone Company quietly removed the phone booth. The company said that visitors were causing too much stress on the environment. Fans of the booth protested, insisting that the phone booth had become a work of art. Later, a plaque was placed at the site as a tribute, but it also vanished. In the end, the phone booth left no trace on the desert that had hosted it. Fans of the phone booth, however, can still hear the dial tone in their hearts.

SKILL PRACTICE Read the item. Write your response.

1. Why was this considered the world's loneliest phone booth?

2. How did the phone booth develop a fan following?

3. Make an inference about the types of stress the visitors caused in the Mojave Desert.

STRATEGY PRACTICE Make a timeline of the Mojave phone booth's most important dates.

Fact and Opinion

WEEK 8 DAY 4

READ THE PASSAGE Think about the facts and opinions that the author expresses about peppers.

How Hot Is That Pepper?

If you love hot, spicy foods, you probably love hot peppers! The spiciness in peppers is determined by special chemicals. If a pepper has a lot of these chemicals, it will be hot.

The heat in peppers is measured using the Scoville scale, which is named after the man who invented it, Wilbur Scoville. Bell peppers are at the bottom of the scale because they don't have much of the chemical that makes peppers hot. Pepperoncini (pep-ur-ohn-CHEE-nee), which usually are pickled, are somewhat hotter than bell peppers. Spicier still are Anaheim and poblano peppers, which are good for mild sauces or for roasting and stuffing with cheese. Then there's the famous jalapeño pepper, found in spicy dishes worldwide. With a Scoville heat unit (SHU) rating of 2,500 to 8,000, this little green pepper makes salsas sing with flavor.

Many peppers are hotter than the jalapeño, but not many mouths can tolerate peppers that have the highest Scoville ratings. Some yellow Hungarian wax peppers are nearly twice as hot as a jalapeño. Cayenne pepper, often sold in powder form, can be 10 times as hot. But even these peppers pale in comparison to the ghost chili pepper.

The ghost chili pepper, which comes from India, currently holds the record as the hottest pepper in the world, with a Scoville rating of over one million. Some farmers in Africa grow these peppers around their crops to keep wild elephants out of their fields. Now that's a powerful pepper!

SKILL PRACTICE Read the item. Write your response.

1. What does the Scoville scale measure?

___

2. What is the SHU of the ghost chili pepper?

___

3. Which peppers are pickled and how hot are they?

___

STRATEGY PRACTICE What questions do you still have about spicy peppers? Write one.

___

Cause and Effect — **WEEK 8**
Fact and Opinion — **DAY 5**

READ THE PASSAGE Think about what happens to Deisha and why.

Good Luck Charm

Deisha paced back and forth as she waited backstage. This would be her most important piano performance yet. At ten years old, she was the youngest performer in the recital. She had practiced playing her song more than 30 times that week. When she closed her eyes at night, the music played over and over again in her head.

Now that the day had arrived, Deisha was not sure she was ready. She smoothed her hair and picked a piece of lint from the new dress that her mother had bought for her. She noticed that her hands were shaking. How could she play the notes of the song if her hands were shaking? She tried to concentrate on steadying them, but they only shook more.

Deisha's piano teacher, Ms. Neal, leaned down to speak to her. "I have something for you," she said, pressing a smooth black stone into Deisha's hand. "It's a special stone. There's no other one like it in the world. You've practiced so much, you don't need anything else."

The stage lights reflected off the polished rock. "Thank you," Deisha said.

When Deisha's name was called, she rubbed the stone, stepped onto the stage, and played better than ever. After her performance, she noticed that Ms. Neal had a whole bag of black stones. "Why did you say this one was so special?" she asked.

Her teacher responded, "Because, like your talent, it belongs only to you."

SKILL PRACTICE Read the item. Write your response.

1. Write two reasons for Deisha's good performance.

___

2. Why does Deisha hear piano music as she falls asleep?

___

3. Why do Deisha's hands shake prior to her performance?

___

STRATEGY PRACTICE Write a short summary that tells the main message of the story.

___

Compare and Contrast — WEEK 9 DAY 1

READ THE PASSAGE Compare how the three students in the story work on a group science project.

The Egg Drop

Marisol, Jack, and Ramon met after school to work on their group science project. Their assignment was to find a way to protect an egg from breaking as it was dropped from a two-story building. Marisol and Ramon were busy working with their materials, which included a pile of newspapers, some bubble wrap, and rubber bands. Marisol was tearing newspaper into strips and watching Jack doodle in a notebook. Finally, she couldn't stay quiet any longer.

"Jack, when are you going to help us?" she asked. "We need to get this project done today."

Ramon reached across the table for another rubber band to weave into the rubber mat he was trying to make. "Yeah, Jack," he said. "Could you put down your cartoons and help us?" Jack was a good friend, but he didn't seem to give science class the same attention that Ramon and Marisol did. His mind always seemed to be somewhere else—mainly in his notebook.

Jack looked up so slowly that Marisol and Ramon thought he may not have heard them at all. Then he turned the page toward them. Jack had sketched a diagram that showed an egg in the center of a layer of newspaper and bubble wrap. The egg had been wrapped with several rubber bands, which crisscrossed each other to make a thick layer of padding. Marisol and Ramon were impressed.

"I was just brainstorming," Jack said. "Do you think it'll work?"

SKILL PRACTICE Read the item. Write your response.

1. Why is this science project challenging?

2. How does Jack's way of working on the project differ from his partners' way?

3. What do Marisol and Ramon think of Jack's idea? Cite text evidence in your response.

STRATEGY PRACTICE Describe a group project you worked on, and compare your group to Jack's.

Compare and Contrast — WEEK 9, DAY 2

READ THE PASSAGE Compare Larry Walters' flight with what you know about flying.

The Lawn Chair Flyer

Larry Walters was a truck driver who always dreamed of flying. When he couldn't get into the U.S. Air Force, he came up with a new plan. One sunny day in July of 1982, Larry made history when he took flight in a homemade aircraft near Los Angeles, California.

Larry tied 45 weather balloons to a lawn chair and used helium tanks to fill the balloons. Sitting in his sturdy chair like the proud captain of a ship, he ordered his friends to cut the anchor rope. But instead of rising slowly to a height of 100 feet (30 m) as he had expected, Larry's aircraft rushed skyward. It rose to over 16,000 feet (4,877 m) in the air. The truck driver with no flight experience was suddenly in airplane territory—in a lawn chair!

Fortunately, Larry had brought along a pellet gun and a two-way radio. He used the radio to communicate with surprised emergency officials. He also shot a few balloons with the pellet gun to lower his aircraft. However, the lawn chair eventually drifted into some power lines, causing a power outage in the nearby city of Long Beach.

After his historic flight, Larry had to pay a fine to the Federal Aviation Administration (FAA) for flying an uncertified aircraft. He complained that the Wright brothers, inventors of the first airplane, had also flown uncertified aircraft. Later, Larry said, "I fulfilled my dream. But I wouldn't do this again for anything."

SKILL PRACTICE Read the item. Write your response.

1. How is Larry similar to the Wright brothers?

2. Why does the author compare Larry to the captain of a ship?

3. Name two ways in which Larry's flight was different from what he had envisioned.

STRATEGY PRACTICE What materials did Larry Walters use for his flight? Use your notes to help you.

Make Inferences — Week 9, Day 3

READ THE PASSAGE — Use clues from the text and what you know about Earth's crust to understand what scientists learned from the Kola Superdeep Borehole.

Underground Mysteries

You may think that our knowledge of Earth is as solid as the ground beneath our feet. However, although scientists know some important facts about Earth's crust, many details are a mystery. To solve some of those mysteries, a group of Russian scientists drilled the deepest hole on the planet. Starting in 1970, researchers and special drillers began digging and drilling a hole in the northwestern part of Russia, on the Kola Peninsula. Before they were done, the Kola Superdeep Borehole was more than 7.5 miles (12 km) deep.

Researchers unearthed many fascinating facts. Miles below the surface, they found rock that was full of water, like a sponge. Scientists believed that the water had formed from extreme pressure inside the rock. The researchers also found a layer of tiny fossils about four miles down, deeper than anyone expected to find fossils. Another surprise was that Earth became much hotter—over 350°F (177°C)—as drillers dug deeper.

Eventually, the drilling area became so hot that the drill bits melted. New holes would close as soon as they were dug. Realizing that better technology was needed, the team stopped drilling in 1992. The deepest hole ever drilled by humans was abandoned, but researchers at new sites continue to investigate the mysteries within Earth's crust.

SKILL PRACTICE — Read the item. Write your response.

1. Why were scientists able to learn new things from the Kola Superdeep Borehole?

2. What made the team realize they needed better technology to continue their work?

3. Why is it important to learn about Earth's crust?

STRATEGY PRACTICE — List two facts that you knew about Earth's crust before reading the passage.

Make Inferences — Week 9, Day 4

READ THE PASSAGE Look for clues about what makes Fabergé eggs special.

A Surprising Present

The year was 1885, and Czar (ZAHR) Alexander III, the ruler of Russia, had an idea for a gift that would surprise and delight his wife, Maria. The traditional Easter gift in Russia was an egg. But Alexander didn't want to give her an ordinary chicken egg.

When Maria saw the gift, she was astonished. The egg that Alexander had given her was about 2½ inches (6 cm) tall and looked simple from the outside. When the czarina (zah-REE-nuh) opened the egg, though, she found a "yolk" made of gold. Inside the hollow yolk was a small golden hen resting on a bed of golden straw. Inside the hen was a miniature diamond crown and a tiny ruby egg. Truly this was a gift made for royalty.

The egg's creator, Peter Carl Fabergé (FAB-ur-ZHAY), enjoyed a lifetime of success as an artist after that. Every year, Fabergé made at least one "imperial egg" for the royal family. Because of the rare materials chosen and the delicate craftsmanship required, each egg often took an entire year to create.

During World War I and the Russian Revolution, some of the eggs were lost. However, Fabergé's remaining eggs are now highly desired collector's items for museums and art lovers around the world. Nine of the imperial eggs sold for 90 million dollars in 2004!

SKILL PRACTICE Read the item. Write your response.

1. How much was each of the Fabergé eggs worth in 2004? How can you tell?

2. What makes Fabergé eggs so valuable?

3. *Each year a new egg is still made for the Russian royal family.* Is this statement true? Cite text evidence in your response.

STRATEGY PRACTICE Circle the words in the passage that helped you figure out the main idea of the passage.

Compare and Contrast — **WEEK 9**
Make Inferences — **DAY 5**

READ THE PASSAGE Compare the two accounts of a hardworking monkey named Mani.

An Unusual Goat Herder

There's a quiet farm in southern India with a most unusual goat herder. She is Mani, a monkey who came to the farm on her own and stayed to do an important job protecting the goats.

The farm grows coffee, oranges, and a spice called cardamom (CAR-duh-mum). The farm is also home to about 75 goats. These playful creatures usually need a human's watchful eye to make sure they don't get lost. At this farm, though, Mani does the daily work of herding the goats.

When Mani first came to the farm, she was injured. The owners nursed her back to health and tried to set her free. Instead of leaving, however, Mani befriended the goats. She takes the goats out to pasture every morning and watches over them until they all return in the evening.

Special Skills

Although Mani cannot speak, this goat-herding monkey uses sounds and gestures to accomplish her duties. When a goat is lost or in danger, Mani alerts the farmers by making a warning sound. Mani's tree-climbing skills really come in handy. When goats can't reach the fruit growing on a high branch, Mani climbs the tree and pulls the branch lower.

Mani has become a regular member of the farm team. She even brings her baby to work every day. She and her baby play with the goats and ride on their backs as they wander to the fields to eat. The farm owners trust Mani to supervise the 75 goats as well as any human could.

SKILL PRACTICE Read the item. Write your response.

1. How is Mani similar to a human goat herder?

   _____
   _____

2. What do both accounts emphasize about Mani?

   _____
   _____

3. Are monkeys native to India? Cite text evidence in your response.

   _____

STRATEGY PRACTICE If you had a monkey helper like Mani, what could she do to help you at home or school?

   _____
   _____

WEEK 10
Character and Setting **DAY 1**

READ THE PASSAGE Think about the two people in the story and where the event takes place.

Grand Opening

Jess's brother Ted had told her that the new city gymnasium was nice, but this was better than anything she could have imagined. The two-story ceiling of the gym was high enough to allow for a tall climbing wall. Dozens of sports balls of all kinds lined the south wall, each kind in its own special rack. Three full-sized basketball courts were filled with kids playing pickup games.

"Pretty awesome, isn't it?" Ted asked. Jess's mouth hung open. She was speechless. Ted waved his hand in front of her face. "Yo, Jess? Isn't it cool?"

"It's perfect," Jess managed to say. She was checking out the volleyball court. Jess loved lots of sports, but volleyball was her favorite. The new net was just waiting for the first spike.

Ted continued, "You can practice your volleyball serves, and I can work on my basketball layups—well, when the crowd thins out, anyway. If we come here every day this summer, tryouts this fall will be a snap."

Jess nodded as she tried to take it all in. Smiling, Ted turned his eyes to the soccer balls. "Or maybe we could kick a soccer ball around while we wait for the courts to clear," he said. "That is, if you're ready to eat my dust!" He made a sudden move toward the balls.

Startled out of her visions of volleyball glory, Jess turned and sprinted ahead of Ted. "Oh yeah?" she called over her shoulder. "You'll never get past me!"

SKILL PRACTICE Read the item. Write your response.

1. Where does this story take place?

   _____

   _____

2. Which two sports are probably Ted's favorites? How can you tell?

   _____

   _____

3. Draw two conclusions about the characters in this text.

   _____

   _____

STRATEGY PRACTICE The story begins with many details of the gym. How do they help tell the story?

_____

_____

WEEK 10
Character and Setting **DAY 2**

READ THE PASSAGE Think about Marie Marvingt's traits and what made them special for the time period in which she lived.

The Amazing Flying Marie

In October 1909, the cold wind whipped across the English Channel. A 34-year-old French woman strapped on a helmet, stepped into a hot-air balloon, and made history. That was how Marie Marvingt became the first woman to fly a balloon over the English Channel. The following year, she became the third woman in the world to earn her pilot's license.

Marie may have been happier in the air than she was on the ground. She began flying at a time when flying was for either the very brave or the very foolish. Nevertheless, she flew as a bomber pilot and as a reporter in World War I. As a trained nurse, Marie also delivered medical supplies and rescued injured soldiers with her airplane.

In those days, flying was more dangerous than it is now. But Marie knew the risks. Her tiny one-person airplane would rise and drop with the wind, like a bird in a storm. She knew how to take control and steer the airplane through rough weather. Flying through the wind and rain were all part of the adventure of early air travel.

In addition to being a pioneer in aviation, Marie was also one of the longest-flying pilots. At age 80, in 1955, Marie learned how to fly a helicopter. She proved to the world that she could be at home in any aircraft, at any age.

SKILL PRACTICE Read the item. Write your response.

1. Which sentence tells the reader that Marie was a skillful pilot? Use quotation marks in your response.

___

2. What was dangerous about flying a plane during World War I?

___

3. Name two adjectives that describe Marie Marvingt. Explain your choices.

___

STRATEGY PRACTICE How did you visualize Marie Marvingt? Describe the picture in your mind.

___

READ THE PASSAGE Think about the main message of the passage.

Prometheus Defeated

In the summer of 1964, a scientist cut down a tree in Nevada. The event started a debate about the importance of scientific study versus protecting the environment. The tree, a bristlecone pine, was the oldest living thing in the world. Some people called the tree "Prometheus," after a tragic hero in Greek mythology. Others knew it as "WPN-114." The two names show how different communities of people felt about the tree.

WPN-114 was likely a seedling around 3100 BC. Scientists knew that the tree was old. They just didn't know how old. But they knew they could find out by examining the tree rings, which form every year inside the trunk. Scientists argued that there was no other way to get valuable information about different time periods long ago. They believed that the knowledge they could gain by cutting down the tree was worth sacrificing it. In fact, scientists did learn a lot.

On the other side of the debate were people who loved the tree as a part of nature. Destroying the tree, they thought, was a horrible mistake. In *The Sierra Club Bulletin,* wilderness photographer Galen Rowell argued that "the wood belonged in the mountains." Friends of the tree used words such as *murder* to describe what was done to Prometheus. To them, the knowledge gained by cutting down the tree wasn't worth the loss. They believed that experiencing the tree alive, as the oldest living link to the past, was equally important.

SKILL PRACTICE Read the item. Write your response.

1. What is this text's theme?

___

___

2. "The two names show how different communities of people felt about the tree." What did the author mean by this sentence?

___

3. With whom do you agree: the scientists who cut down the tree or the naturalists who protested its death? Why?

___

___

STRATEGY PRACTICE How does the author use a compare-and-contrast structure to present the debate?

___

___

WEEK 10 — Theme — DAY 4

READ THE PASSAGE Think about the message of the story.

Practice Makes Perfect

Minh was excited when his grandmother invited him into her pottery studio. After all, Nana did not give all her grandchildren such an invitation. Minh looked forward to sinking his hands into some wet clay and placing his bowl in the heated kiln until it hardened like stone.

"Be careful with that," Nana said as Minh picked up one of the bowls. The boy gently put the bowl back on the shelf and stuck his hands inside his pockets. He was anxious to get started on the lesson Nana had promised him. And he didn't want to risk losing that chance by breaking any of her finished pieces of pottery.

Five hours later, Minh was frustrated and tired. His first attempt, a black blob that looked more like a rock than a bowl, was a failure. His second attempt was hardly any better. However, he had at least figured out how to make a smooth opening in the center of the clay. Meanwhile, Nana was keeping busy. A wide, shallow bowl and a deep, narrow bowl rested on Nana's worktable. Her practiced hands began to shape yet another spinning lump of clay. "I'll never get it!" Minh said, watching her work.

Nana looked at her grandson and sighed. "Don't worry, you'll get it," she reassured him. "The only way you won't learn is if you give up."

SKILL PRACTICE Read the item. Write your response.

1. What theme does the title suggest?

___

2. Does Minh appreciate Nana's pottery-making skills? Explain.

___

3. How do Minh's feelings change from the start of the story to the end?

___

STRATEGY PRACTICE Underline the words that helped you visualize Nana's studio. Describe it.

___

Character and Setting — **WEEK 10**
Theme — **DAY 5**

READ THE PASSAGE   Think about the location featured in the passage, and look for details that tell you what the author believes about nature.

The Old Man of Crater Lake

Oregon's Crater Lake—or, rather, the site for this deep, clear lake—was once a volcano. The lake formed when the peak of the volcano caved in and the hole filled up with rain and snow. The area is now home to diverse wildlife, evergreen forests, and chilly mountain water. The lake also boasts an unusual feature: a 30-foot-tall (9-meter-tall) tree stump, known as the Old Man of the Lake, that rises out of the water about four feet (1.2 meters) above the surface.

The Old Man of the Lake is special for a few reasons. First, it floats vertically, bobbing up and down in the water and moving freely across the lake. Second, it has been there since at least 1896! The lake's cold water has preserved the wood. But how does the long stump float upright? Scientists think that when the tree tumbled into the lake long ago, rocks were probably wedged inside its root system. They served as weights, holding the root end of the tree underwater.

Because the Old Man drifts all over the lake, boaters alert each other about its location. Scientists have tried tying up the stump to keep it in place. But they noticed that whenever the Old Man was tied up, bad weather arrived. When they released the stump, the weather improved. This strange coincidence is one of the many intriguing things that bring visitors to Crater Lake.

Although the Old Man of the Lake remains a mystery to visitors, one thing is certain. This fascinating piece of floating wood—and the legendary waters that surround it—are examples of nature's beauty and strength.

SKILL PRACTICE   Read the item. Write your response.

1. What is the theme of this text?

_____

_____

2. Write two reasons why the Old Man of the Lake is mysterious.

_____

3. In what way does the main character in this text differ from typical main characters?

_____

STRATEGY PRACTICE   How do the ideas in each paragraph lead up to the main message?

_____

_____

Author's Purpose — WEEK 11, DAY 1

READ THE PASSAGE Think about why the author wrote this passage about the world's slowest song.

The Slowest Song in the World

Life moves fast these days. With supersonic trains, high-speed Internet, and microwave meals, people no longer slow down and experience life the way they used to. Maybe that's what composer John Cage was thinking when he wrote "As Slow As Possible." The musical piece, written for piano or organ, is about as far as you can get from an upbeat, high-energy tune. Cage's directions to musicians were to play the piece as slowly as they could. Usually, the piece lasts about twenty minutes. An organist in Baltimore, though, managed to stretch "As Slow As Possible" to nearly 15 hours.

John Cage wanted people to really hear the music being played. That was his goal. But can you imagine sitting through a fifteen-hour concert? You could eat three meals or sleep a full night in the same amount of time! That's not even the longest performance, either.

An electronic church organ in Germany has been programmed to play "As Slow As Possible" over a period of 639 years. The piece began in the year 2001. However, because the piece begins with a long musical rest, or pause, the first notes did not play until 2003. This is the longest and slowest piece of music in history so far, and it will not be over for many generations. What will the world look like when "As Slow As Possible" finally ends? And who will be listening?

SKILL PRACTICE Read the item. Write your response.

1. What is the author's purpose for writing this text?

2. What is the author's goal in the second paragraph?

3. Why did the author end the text with two questions?

STRATEGY PRACTICE Write one question you had while reading the passage. If you found the answer, write it, too.

Author's Purpose — WEEK 11, DAY 2

READ THE PASSAGE Think about why the author wrote the story about Emma and Martha.

Disturbing the Peace

It was a beautiful spring morning on Lake Powell. Birds chirped and the trees rustled in the chilly morning breeze. Gentle waves moved along the surface of the clear blue water. Emma sat on the dock with her history book in her lap, occasionally looking out at the peaceful lake.

Suddenly, running footsteps came from behind and a voice shouted, "Kowabunga!" Before Emma could move an inch, her best friend Martha flew directly over her head. Martha was shrieking with laughter as she dove into the water. The cold water splashed all over Emma and soaked her.

As Martha swam back to the dock, Emma was wiping her face. "You said you'd never do that again!" Emma declared.

Martha raked the hair out of her eyes and shrugged. "I said I wouldn't splash you at the pool, Em. We're at a lake now. And, come on, how much studying do you need to do on this trip? You've been reading all morning." Martha splashed the water playfully. "Come on, jump in! The water's great."

Emma sighed and closed her book. She would have to learn about pioneers along the Oregon Trail another day. The cool spring air was giving way to the summer sun. And besides, her best friend was just begging to be beaten in a race across the lake.

SKILL PRACTICE Read the item. Write your response.

1. Why does the author describe the setting in the first paragraph?

2. What does the author want you to think about Martha?

3. What will probably happen next? How do you know?

STRATEGY PRACTICE Write about a time when someone disturbed a peaceful moment that you were enjoying.

WEEK 11 — Prediction — DAY 3

READ THE PASSAGE Look for clues to predict what you will learn about Bouvet Island.

The Loneliest Island

In the middle of the frigid South Atlantic Ocean, one island stands alone. It lies near Antarctica. But it is far enough away that early explorers had difficulty finding it. At about four miles (6.4 km) long, the island is covered in glaciers. It is home to an inactive volcano and huge amounts of ice. The steep cliffs that surround the island make sea landings almost impossible. This is Bouvet Island, the loneliest island in the world.

A French explorer discovered Bouvet Island in 1739, but the island was so difficult to approach that nobody set foot on it for nearly a hundred years. No people live on Bouvet Island, and little vegetation grows there. Seals come and go, but they haven't seen humans since seal hunting and whaling stopped in the area. The island is cold year-round, with an average temperature of about 29°F (–1.7°C).

In recent years, Bouvet Island has had a little more contact with the world. Norway, which claimed the island in 1928, set up an unmanned weather station there in 1977. Today, this quiet island near the South Pole sends weather data to a satellite, which transmits the information to researchers in Norway. Scientists learn more every day about the island and its surroundings. Meanwhile, Bouvet Island stands strong and silent in the harsh climate.

SKILL PRACTICE Read the item. Write your response.

1. Write two predictions you made as soon as you read the title.

2. How do the island's physical features keep it a lonely place?

3. Draw a conclusion about why Norway claimed Bouvet Island.

STRATEGY PRACTICE Write two questions you would like to ask an explorer of Bouvet Island.

Week 11 — Prediction — Day 4

READ THE PASSAGE Look for clues to predict what you will learn about the town of Centralia.

A Unique Ghost Town

Centralia, Pennsylvania, used to be an ordinary town. Nestled in an area known for its coal mining history, the town offered job opportunities and a pleasant place to live. It had good schools and a fine local library. Things started to change, though, in the 1960s. Below the surface, Centralia was anything but normal. Now most of the town is gone.

In 1962, a burning landfill sparked an underground blaze. One of the veins of coal that runs beneath the town caught fire. Unlike fires above ground, this slow-burning fire crept along as it found more coal to burn. As the fire spread beneath the town, the ground began to open up and release poisonous gases. Basements filled with smoke and hot gas. Several efforts were made to stop the fire. All of them failed.

Eventually, it was clear that the fire was not going to die out. In fact, the Centralia mine fire is expected to burn for about 250 years. When the people who lived there became aware of the danger they were in, many of them left town for good. But others wanted to stay.

The town's highway, which cracked open from the mine fire, was closed. The government decided to buy the homes in town and destroy them. The only homes left were those occupied by residents who refused to leave. Today, people sometimes visit the area and take photos to show how Centralia has changed. But a few residents have held on to the history of a town now long gone, with a future that exists only in their imaginations.

SKILL PRACTICE Read the item. Write your response.

1. What should occur in Centralia in about 200 years?

2. Is Centralia a typical ghost town? Explain.

3. What do you think will happen to the people who refuse to leave Centralia?

STRATEGY PRACTICE What ghost towns have you heard of or seen in movies? Explain to a partner how those towns remind you of Centralia.

Author's Purpose — **WEEK 11**
Prediction — **DAY 5**

READ THE PASSAGE Think about why the author wrote the story, and use clues to predict what will happen.

The Amazing Phil

Sasha had simply wanted to get out of the car and stretch her legs. When she and her mom drove up to the ancient-looking gas station, neither of them was prepared to come face to face with a dinosaur. The sculpture loomed 20 feet (6 m) over the car. It was a *T. rex,* and the green paint was peeling from its front legs, which dangled in the air. Sasha's mom wasn't sure what to make of the whole thing. "I wonder who created this," she said, shading her eyes from the bright sun.

"I did," said a shaky voice nearby. Sasha turned around to see an elderly man propped up on a cane. He steadied himself and pointed one finger up toward the *T. rex* sculpture. "He's the Amazing Phil," the man said. "I built him in 1955, right after I opened the gas station. He brought in a crowd for a long time, back when people didn't drive so fast." The man's weathered face broke into a soft smile.

"It's a great sculpture," Sasha's mom half-lied. "I like the colors. So, what's your name?"

"My name's Phil, too," said the man. He leaned back on his cane. "My wife is inside. She just made a pecan pie. Do you ladies like pie?"

Sasha looked at her mom. Her mom looked up at the dinosaur and then gazed up the road for a few awkward seconds. Then she smiled and looked at Phil. "Pecan pie is our favorite," she replied, closing the car door behind her.

SKILL PRACTICE Read the item. Write your response.

1. Why does the author include the detail about the sculpture's peeling paint?

2. Why does Sasha's mom "gaze up the road for a few awkward seconds"?

3. What will probably happen next?

STRATEGY PRACTICE Write one question you have about the *T. rex* sculpture or another part of the story.

Nonfiction Text Features — WEEK 12, DAY 1

READ THE INFORMATION Think about the features of the index page and how the excerpt relates to it.

INDEX (continued)

catalogs, clothing, *22, 77*

Chanel, Coco, *84–86*

children's fashions:
  aprons, pinafores, *12, 28*
  dresses, *15*
  jeans, *46*
  sailor suits, *23*

cotton, *14–18, 28, 45*

department stores, *24, 87*

designers:
  Chanel, Coco, *84–86*
  Dior, Christian, *87, 90*
  St. Laurent, Yves, *91*
  Wang, Vera, *101*
  Worth, Charles, *20, 82*

Dior, Christian, *87, 90*

dresses:
  girls', *15*
  women's, *32–34, 101*

fabric:
  cotton, *14–18, 28, 45*
  synthetic fabrics, *99*
  wool, *12, 28*

fashion magazines, *22, 55, 102–103*

fashion schools, *75, 93*

hairstyles, *19, 26, 40, 53, 67, 80, 98, 102*

hats, *19, 23, 71, 84*

Gabrielle "Coco" Chanel was born in 1883 in a small French town. Her family was poor. Her mother died of tuberculosis in 1895. Her father then left the family to find work.

Chanel spent six years in an orphanage, where she learned to sew. It was a humble beginning for a woman who would change the fashion world forever.

At 18 years old, Chanel left the orphanage and became a singer. She performed in clubs throughout France. It was during this time that she got the nickname "Coco."

When she moved to Paris, Chanel learned to make hats. She opened her first fashion store in 1910. Soon she started making clothes and then opened two more stores. In the 1920s, Chanel introduced her first perfume.

SKILL PRACTICE Read the item. Write your response.

1. Which entry in the index would lead you to the excerpt on the right? What would be the page number?

_____

_____

2. On what page(s) would you expect to read about the Fashion Institute of Technology located in New York City?

_____

_____

3. What are the two index entries associated with page 45?

_____

_____

STRATEGY PRACTICE Make a timeline of Coco Chanel's life, based on the passage.

Nonfiction Text Features — WEEK 12, DAY 2

READ THE INTERVIEW Notice how the interview is organized to show who is speaking.

Recently, *Dog Days* magazine had a chance to talk with trainer Mary Fineday at the Bloomsday Dog Show in Rochester, New York.

Dog Days: Thank you for meeting with us on such a busy day. We're really enjoying the Bloomsday Dog Show, and we can't wait to meet your dogs. Can you tell us a little about what you're doing right now?

Mary Fineday: Gladly. I'm brushing Anna, my Norfolk terrier. Her golden fur can easily get dirty when she runs around. We want to make sure she looks perfect for the competition. That means a lot of brushing.

Dog Days: How long have you had Anna?

Mary Fineday: She's three and a half years old, and we've raised her from the day she was born. She eats the finest cuts of meat and exercises on a track that was built just for her.

Dog Days: That's one lucky dog! Does Anna enjoy the dog show as much as you do?

Mary Fineday: Anna has a great time. She loves the attention and the chance to show the judges her skills. She's trained to run and jump at exactly the right time, and she loves the workout. She knows she'll get a treat if she does well.

Dog Days: You get a nice treat, too—$50,000—if Anna wins.

Mary Fineday: It's true. If we win, we'll donate $10,000 of the prize money to various dog charities. The rest of it will go toward taking care of Anna and the other dogs at our dog club.

SKILL PRACTICE Read the item. Write your response.

1. How does the image support the text?

2. What is the purpose of the third question the interviewer asks?

3. How can you tell that this magazine is *not* read exclusively by Norfolk terrier owners?

STRATEGY PRACTICE Continue the interview. Write the next question you would ask if you were the interviewer. Then write Mary's response.

Visual Information — WEEK 12, DAY 3

READ THE MAP Think about what the map tells you.

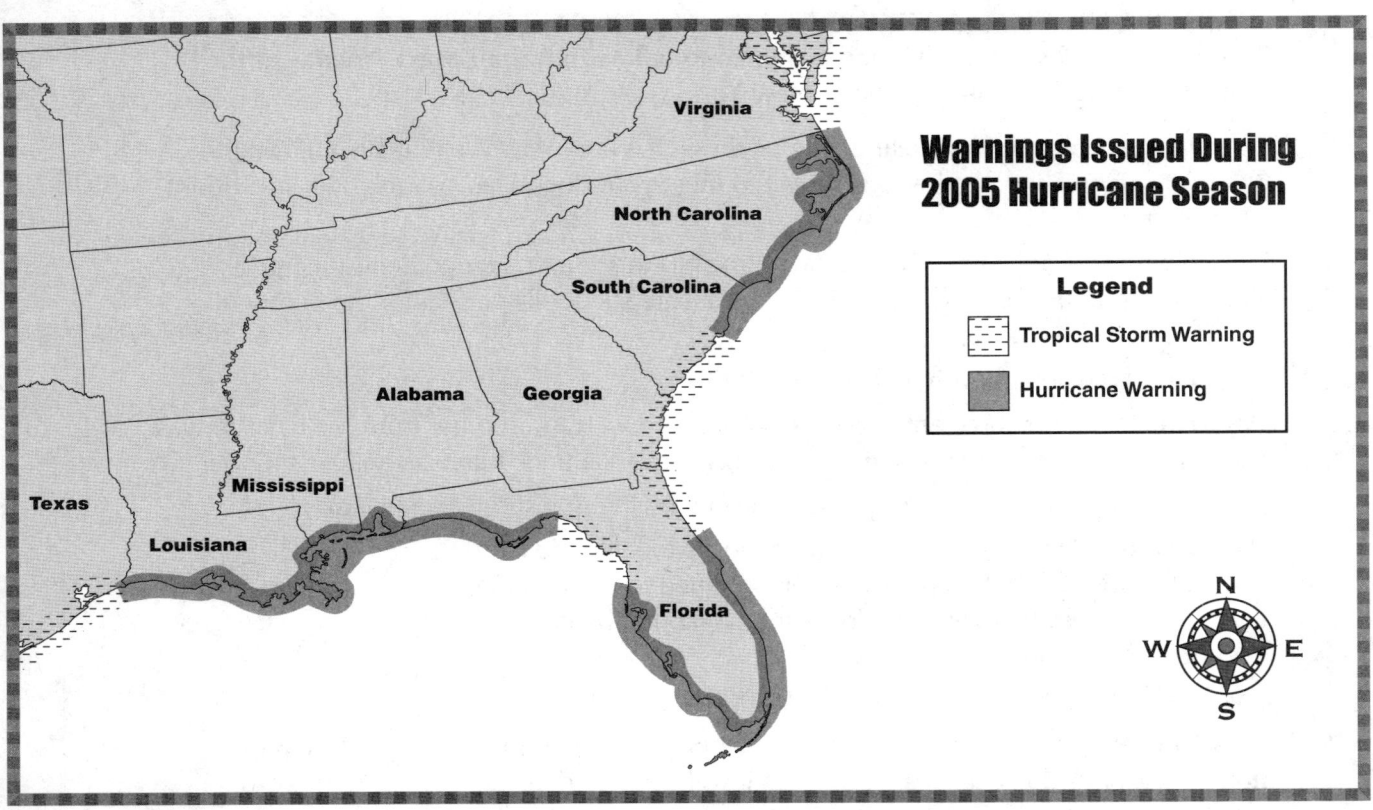

SKILL PRACTICE Read the item. Write your response.

1. Name the two states that had both kinds of warnings in 2005.

   _____

   _____

2. How does this map change from year to year? How does it stay the same?

   _____

   _____

3. From the map you can infer that hurricanes come from which two directions?

   _____

STRATEGY PRACTICE Explain in your own words how to use the legend on the map.

   _____

   _____

Visual Information — WEEK 12 DAY 4

READ THE GRAPH Think about how the graph presents data on education and earnings.

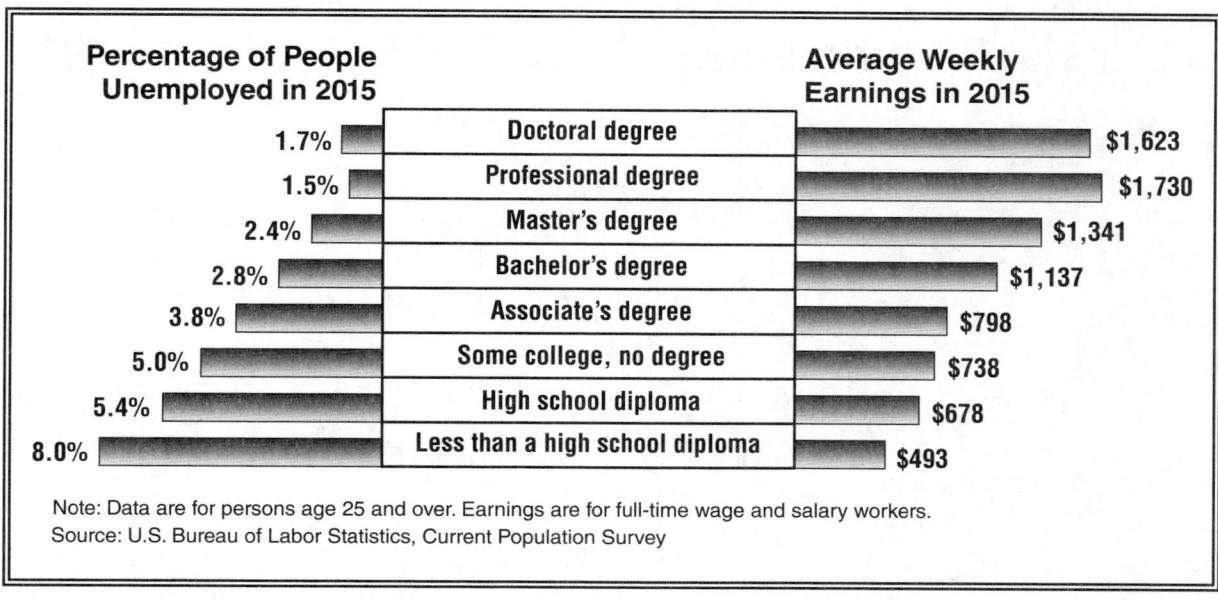

Education Pays

A person's ability to get a job is related to his or her level of education. Likewise, the amount of money that people earn is usually related to the amount of education they have had.

Percentage of People Unemployed in 2015	Degree	Average Weekly Earnings in 2015
1.7%	Doctoral degree	$1,623
1.5%	Professional degree	$1,730
2.4%	Master's degree	$1,341
2.8%	Bachelor's degree	$1,137
3.8%	Associate's degree	$798
5.0%	Some college, no degree	$738
5.4%	High school diploma	$678
8.0%	Less than a high school diploma	$493

Note: Data are for persons age 25 and over. Earnings are for full-time wage and salary workers.
Source: U.S. Bureau of Labor Statistics, Current Population Survey

SKILL PRACTICE Read the item. Write your response.

1. What was the average weekly earnings of a person with a master's degree in 2015? How does that compare with a person with a high school diploma?

_____

_____

2. Draw two conclusions from studying this graph.

_____

_____

3. Which group of workers had the highest unemployment rate in 2015? How does it relate to the title of the text?

_____

STRATEGY PRACTICE Why do most of the bars on the left side of the graph get shorter as they go up, but the bars on the right side get longer?

_____

_____

Nonfiction Text Features — **WEEK 12**
Visual Information — **DAY 5**

READ THE ADVERTISEMENT Think about the information that is presented in the text and the illustration.

North Bay Tours Presents...

A special 2-hour sunset cruise around Otter Cove!

$59 per person

Price includes:
- A buffet dinner with your choice of beverages and dessert
- A 5" × 7" (13 x 18 cm) photo of you and the crew
- A souvenir pin and mug from North Bay Tours

Boarding begins at 5:00 PM. Departure is at 5:30 PM.

SKILL PRACTICE Read the item. Write your response.

1. What would it cost for a couple to go on this tour? How do you know?

_____
_____

2. When does the tour return to the dock? How do you know?

_____

3. What important pieces of information are missing from the ad?

_____
_____

STRATEGY PRACTICE What information could be added to the ad that would encourage people to sign up for the cruise?

_____
_____

Main Idea and Details — Week 13, Day 1

READ THE PASSAGE — Think about the main idea of the passage and the details that support it.

Born to Ride

In 1995, Miguel Indurain (een-doo-RANE) won the Tour de France for the fifth time in a row. The Tour de France is the most difficult bicycle race in the world. No one before Miguel had ever won five Tour races in a row. What made Miguel such a successful athlete?

Miguel grew up on a farm and learned the value of hard work at an early age. His father taught him that work is something you always do, no matter how difficult it is. Miguel had large lungs and a strong heart, both of which helped him endure the 2,200 miles (3,541 km) of the Tour de France. He was naturally calm, which allowed him to stay focused on the course. And he trained hard, had a good bike, and was surrounded by excellent teammates who helped him succeed.

In addition to the Tour de France, Miguel won the Giro d'Italia, another national bicycle race, in 1992 and 1993. He captured a gold medal in track cycling during the 1996 Olympics in Atlanta, Georgia. Later that year, he retired from competitive racing at the age of 31.

Miguel's long list of accomplishments assures him a place among the top athletes in history. But fans will especially remember his relaxed and friendly attitude. "My strength," Miguel said, "was that I was more balanced than most other riders."

SKILL PRACTICE — Read the item. Write your response.

1. Cite the main idea statement from the text. Use quotation marks.

_____

_____

2. List the years in which Miguel Indurain won the Tour de France.

_____

_____

3. In which years did Indurain win two national bike races?

_____

_____

STRATEGY PRACTICE — List two main reasons that Miguel's fans will remember him.

_____

_____

Main Idea and Details — WEEK 13 DAY 2

READ THE PASSAGE Look for details that help you picture the characters and events in the story.

Natural Entertainment

When the days grew long in the middle of summer, Leticia liked to go to the park, stretch out on her back, and watch the clouds. Sometimes the clouds looked like animals, everyday objects, or people she knew. One thing was certain—clouds never stayed in place for long.

One day, Leticia saw a cloud that looked like a dragon. After a few minutes, it changed from a standing dragon to a flying dragon. Then it appeared to change direction. Another cloud floated in to mix with it, and the dragon turned into a dancing penguin with a hat. Then it turned into a sitting dog, then a barking dog, then an alligator. "This is better than TV!" Leticia proclaimed.

Mr. Espinosa, the music teacher at Leticia's school, was flying a kite with his children at the other end of the park. He recognized Leticia's voice. He gave the spool of kite string to his son and came over to greet Leticia.

"Hi, Mr. Espinosa!" Leticia said. "Look at those clouds. They keep changing! First they looked like a dragon, then a penguin, then a dog, and now an alligator!"

Mr. Espinosa looked up. "An alligator?" he said. "That looks like a speedboat to me."

Leticia looked again. He was right! "How do clouds know how to make so many shapes?"

"It's a mystery," answered Mr. Espinosa. "Definitely better than TV, though."

"Definitely," Leticia said, as the speedboat turned into a chicken.

SKILL PRACTICE Read the item. Write your response.

1. Write the main idea of the text in your own words.
   _____
   _____

2. Why is Mr. Espinosa at the park?
   _____
   _____

3. What shapes have you seen in clouds?
   _____

STRATEGY PRACTICE Explain which cloud description was easiest for you to visualize and why.
   _____
   _____

READ THE PASSAGE — Number the sequence of events at Oak Island as you read.

Underground Secrets

Oak Island lies off the east coast of Nova Scotia, Canada. Some people say that pirate gold is buried there. Others say it's the hiding place for the lost jewels of a former queen of France. Most people who have heard of this place suspect that it holds some kind of treasure.

The legend of the treasure first started in 1795, when a teenager named Daniel McGinnis noticed odd markings on a tree. The marks led him to think a rope had been tied to the tree and used for lowering a weight into a hole. The next day, McGinnis and his friends dug into the ground and uncovered a layer of stones just two feet (0.6 m) down. After that was a barrier of logs every 10 feet (3 m).

Years later, McGinnis returned with a crew. They found even deeper layers of charcoal and clay, as well as a stone tablet with symbols that appeared to be a secret code. The crew continued to dig, but the pit filled up with water and they had to give up. According to the legend, the tablet was later translated. It claimed that a treasure lay 40 feet (12 m) below it!

Since then, others have taken up the search. Around 1970, a team sent a video camera down into the pit, but the images were not clear. Divers also looked for clues, but the water was too dark and cloudy. Maybe one day we will know if the legend of the Oak Island treasure is true.

SKILL PRACTICE — Read the item. Write your response.

1. What did Daniel McGinnis discover first?

2. What is the last thing that McGinnis found before he gave up his search on Oak Island?

3. Why did the video camera and scuba divers fail to find the treasure?

STRATEGY PRACTICE — Look back at the events you numbered. Use them to summarize what happened at Oak Island.

Sequence — WEEK 13 DAY 4

READ THE PASSAGE Read slowly and pay attention to the sequence of events.

The Loneliest Tree

Many centuries ago, the Sahara was full of trees. The climate there was different from what it is now. As time passed, the land became dry and hot, and trees became scarce. But one acacia (uh-KAY-shuh) tree in the Ténéré (TAY-nay-RAY) region of Niger survived longer than the rest.

Caravans transporting goods across the vast expanse of desert used the tree of Ténéré as a landmark. This tree was so important for navigating the sandy landscape that no one dared to cut off its branches for firewood. It was the only tree for almost 250 miles (402 km) around.

In 1938, French military engineers dug a well near the tree. They discovered water more than 100 feet (31 m) underground. That's how deep the roots of the acacia tree had reached to keep itself alive. Unfortunately, one of the military vehicles backed into the tree during the digging operation. The accident damaged one of the tree's main branches.

After World War II, trucks became the main form of transportation for caravans in the area, replacing camels. In 1973, the acacia tree was once again struck by a truck. This time the tree could not withstand the force. The remains of the world's loneliest tree were taken to the Niger National Museum. However, travelers still have a landmark to help them cross the desert. A metal monument now stands where the tree once grew.

SKILL PRACTICE Read the item. Write your response.

1. What occurred as the weather changed in the Sahara Desert?

2. What happened just before the first accident damaged the tree of Ténéré?

3. Why is there a monument where the tree once stood?

STRATEGY PRACTICE Describe what the Sahara probably looked like many centuries ago.

Main Idea and Details — **WEEK 13**
Sequence — **DAY 5**

READ THE PASSAGE Think about the main idea and the sequence of events in the story.

Homemade Pasta

When Darnell and his older sister Lucy found an easy recipe for homemade pasta noodles and tomato sauce, they couldn't wait to try it. Their parents had said they were now old enough to cook dinner for the family, and spaghetti was their favorite food.

First, they made the noodles. They mixed together flour, water, eggs, salt, and a little olive oil to prepare the dough. Lucy used a rolling pin to press the dough flat. Next, she used a knife to carefully cut the dough into thin strips. Then she put the noodles aside for later.

Darnell chopped up a large onion and a bunch of fresh basil leaves. He put a clove of garlic into a small garlic press and smashed the clove. Lucy helped him cook the onions and garlic in some olive oil in a pot. When the onions and garlic were soft and golden, Darnell added a can of crushed tomatoes, the basil, and some salt and pepper. Then he turned the heat down low.

When the sauce was almost ready, Lucy boiled water in a large pot to cook the noodles. Darnell was relieved to find out that fresh pasta cooks much faster than dried pasta from the store. Everyone was very hungry by the time dinner was ready.

"This is delicious!" Mom said. "You two did such a great job."

"Thanks, Mom," Lucy said. "It was pretty easy." Darnell was too busy eating to respond. They both knew that this would not be the last time they made dinner for the family.

SKILL PRACTICE Read the item. Write your response.

1. Write the main idea of the text in your own words.

2. What is the third thing Lucy did to make the noodles?

3. How do you know that making the spaghetti took longer than the siblings had anticipated? Cite text evidence in your response.

STRATEGY PRACTICE Summarize how Lucy and Darnell made dinner.

Cause and Effect — WEEK 14, DAY 1

READ THE PASSAGE Look for factors that explain Cliff Young's victory.

A Real-Life Story of the Tortoise and the Hare

Every year in Australia, the toughest long-distance runners race more than 500 miles (805 km) from Sydney to Melbourne. The race takes more than five days to complete. It attracts world-class athletes—the kind who become spokespeople for sneakers and sports drinks.

In 1983, however, as the competitors lined up to race, they were joined by a 61-year-old farmer wearing overalls and rubber boots. His name was Cliff Young. The other runners thought he was a confused spectator. Cliff assured them that he was there to race. He explained that on his family's sheep farm, he often had to round up 2,000 or so animals by himself. "Sometimes I had to run after those sheep for two or three days," he said.

When the race began, the younger runners flew past Cliff. Instead of chasing after them, Cliff shuffled along in an unusual way. The other runners and the spectators thought he would never finish the race. But something happened. When all the other runners took a break to sleep, Cliff kept running. The other runners caught up to him each morning, but eventually Cliff was too far ahead to be passed. On the fifth day, the sheep farmer shuffled into first place.

Cliff received $10,000 for winning the race. He said he did not realize there would be prize money, and he gave the funds to his fellow runners. Doing this made him a hero in Australia. Since then, many runners have adopted his shuffling stride. No one sleeps during the race anymore, either. The farmer changed long-distance racing and proved that age and style aren't everything.

SKILL PRACTICE Read the item. Write your response.

1. Explain how the author chose the title.

2. How did Cliff Young change long-distance running?

3. Why did the other runners think that Young was a confused spectator?

STRATEGY PRACTICE Describe two important things you would tell someone about Cliff Young.

WEEK 14 — Cause and Effect — DAY 2

READ THE PASSAGE Think about why the artist created Kryptos and the effect it had on people.

Cracking the Code of Kryptos

When the directors of the Central Intelligence Agency (CIA) wanted a piece of art for the courtyard of their new headquarters, they hired artist James Sanborn. In response, Sanborn created a curious sculpture, which he titled Kryptos. *Kryptos* is the Greek word for "hidden," and the sculpture has lived up to its mysterious name.

Kryptos is made out of copper, granite, wood, and other natural materials. The sculpture consists mainly of a giant, curving copper screen with four sections of coded messages. At first, only Sanborn knew the meaning of the messages. To create the code for them, he cut more than 2,000 letters into the metal. He carved ancient symbols and Morse code into the stones surrounding the screen. From the day it was put in place, the sculpture became an object of beauty for visitors and a challenge for code crackers, both inside and outside the CIA.

In 1998, a CIA scientist announced that he had solved some pieces of the code. The next year, a scientist in California made the same claim. The CIA scientist used pencil and paper to figure out the code. The scientist in California used a computer. Their results were similar.

Three of the four sections of code have now been solved. But what happens if the secret code outlives the artist? Will the message stay hidden forever? Sanborn says that he has shared the solution with one other person, just in case. Meanwhile, this work of art remains a beautiful puzzle for code lovers around the world.

SKILL PRACTICE Read the item. Write your response.

1. Why is it appropriate that James Sanborn created Kryptos for the CIA?

2. Why has it taken so long for people to crack Kryptos's code?

3. Why did Sanborn share the solution with another person?

STRATEGY PRACTICE Write a question about the title of the passage. If you found the answer, write it, too.

WEEK 14 — Fact and Opinion — DAY 3

READ THE PASSAGE Think about which details are facts and which express opinions.

The Cathedral of Junk

If you looked over the fence into his messy backyard in Austin, Texas, you might think Vince Hannemann had forgotten to take out the trash for a few years. In fact, Vince has been collecting old kitchen utensils, bottles, lawnmowers, bicycles, and other discarded objects since 1989—all for his "Cathedral of Junk." The structure, which began with a few hubcaps, grew to be over two stories tall before the city of Austin told Vince that he would have to cut it back in order to meet safety codes.

For many years, Vince's Cathedral of Junk was a quirky landmark and a fascinating work of art. Objects of all kinds were wired to the frame of the cathedral, both inside and out. Silvery CDs hung from ceilings made of old golf clubs, bike wheels, and other treasures. Neon lights buzzed softly. In the Cathedral of Junk, there was no such thing as a useless object.

Tourists and fans visited the site daily, even though Vince didn't build it to attract attention. He says he built it just for fun. He called it his clubhouse and loved the fact that other people enjoyed it too. Senior citizens came to explore the place, pointing out collectibles that they might have owned at one time. Vince even allowed couples to get married there.

Some people worried that the building was not stable. Vince tried to calm their fears. "This is built to withstand Texas storms," he said. But in June of 2010, Vince finally gave up trying to meet the city's rules and decided to break the Cathedral down into smaller works of art. Visiting Vince's yard is still worth the trip, though, even if the trash heaps aren't as big.

SKILL PRACTICE Read the item. Write your response.

1. What is Vince Hannemann's opinion about the people who want to visit his yard?

2. In the third paragraph, how many of the sentences are facts? Explain.

3. What is the author's opinion of Hannemann's artwork? Cite text evidence and use quotation marks.

STRATEGY PRACTICE Underline three sentences that contain the most important information for someone to know about the Cathedral of Junk. Then tell a partner why you chose them.

Fact and Opinion

WEEK 14 DAY 4

READ THE PASSAGE   Identify the facts and the opinions about Knut the polar bear.

"Cute Knut" Becomes a Business Bear

In December 2006, a polar bear named Knut (k-NOOT) was born at the Berlin Zoo in Germany. The zookeepers had no idea that this incredibly adorable bear cub would cause such big changes for the zoo.

Knut was different from other polar bears in two ways. First, he was rejected by his mother. She would not care for him or feed him. So Knut was raised by humans. Second, he was remarkably playful with people and very easy to photograph. Knut became the star attraction at the zoo, which earned more money in 2007 than in any other year in its history. The money came from an increase in visitor admissions and from sales of toys, DVDs, and books about Knut. Newspapers dubbed him "Cute Knut," and his photo appeared on magazine covers worldwide.

As time passed, Knut grew bigger. He wasn't as cute anymore. The once-cuddly cub became a full-size bear weighing more than 300 pounds (136 kg)! And as Knut grew, so did his problems. He often cried if nobody stood near his pen. This was a sign that he had become too accustomed to having a crowd around him. Also, zookeepers could no longer get close to Knut. They were concerned that he would accidentally hurt them. Knut continued to live at the zoo for three more years, but he was no longer a star attraction.

On March 19, 2011, Knut passed away unexpectedly. His death caused an outpouring of grief, and thousands of fans visited the zoo to honor him. In October 2012, the zoo unveiled a bronze statue as a tribute to this unique polar bear.

SKILL PRACTICE   Read the item. Write your response.

1. Reread the first paragraph's second sentence. Which words signal that it is an opinion statement?

_____

_____

2. Are there any opinions stated in the last paragraph? Explain.

_____

_____

3. How did Knut financially help the Berlin Zoo?

_____

STRATEGY PRACTICE   Write a question about Knut based on the information in the passage. Then have a partner answer the question.

_____

Cause and Effect — **WEEK 14**
Fact and Opinion — **DAY 5**

READ THE PASSAGE Look for clues that tell you what happened with Tom and Lindsey before the beginning of the story.

In the Cafeteria

When Tom brought his lunch to her table, Lindsey knew something was up. "Your friends are over there," she said, nodding toward the other side of the cafeteria.

"I'd rather sit here today," Tom replied. He took a bite out of his pizza and looked around the cafeteria. Lindsey stared straight ahead, silent.

"So, what's new?" Tom asked. Lindsey picked at her food, pretending that she hadn't heard him. "Look, Lindsey, I'm sorry," Tom said. "I was just kidding about your shoes."

"I can't believe you said that in front of everyone," Lindsey said. Anger rose inside her, but she kept control of herself. "My mom bought me those shoes because she thought I would like them. Now everyone's going to call me 'Sparkle Toes' forever." She pushed her feet beneath her backpack, which she had placed on the floor. She tried her best to hide the silver sneakers with their glittery pink laces. "I thought we were friends," she said, looking down.

"We *are* friends," Tom said. "I was just trying to be funny. How can I make it up to you?"

Finally Lindsey realized that Tom meant what he said. Plus, she had an idea. She began unlacing her shoes. "Give me your laces. You wear mine for the rest of the day," she said. Then she glanced at the second piece of pizza on Tom's plate. "And give me your other slice of pizza. Then we'll be even."

Tom nodded and smiled. "That seems fair," he said, pushing his plate toward Lindsey with one hand and reaching down to untie his laces with the other.

SKILL PRACTICE Read the item. Write your response.

1. Why does Tom sit with Lindsey at lunchtime?

___

___

2. Why do Lindsey and Tom exchange shoelaces?

___

___

3. Cite an opinion that Lindsey states. Use quotation marks.

___

STRATEGY PRACTICE What happened before the story began? Tell a partner how you figured it out.

Compare and Contrast — WEEK 15, DAY 1

READ THE PASSAGE Think about how the two science fair projects are alike and different.

Two Volcanoes

Lea thought there was a good chance that her volcano project would win first place at the science fair. She had covered a glass tube with a cone-shaped wire frame and plaster. Then she had painted it brown so the cone looked like a mountain. When it was her turn to present her project, she would put baking soda in the glass tube and add vinegar to it. The vinegar and acid would cause a chemical reaction, and the mixture would bubble up out of the top. She even added red food coloring to the vinegar to make the mixture look like hot lava. The handwritten notecards next to the model on the display explained how a volcano erupts.

Bernadette thought it was very likely that *her* volcano would win first place at the science fair. She had sculpted a mountain from brown clay and had shaped pieces of red, orange, and black clay to represent lava flowing down the sides. She had even formed small rocks and trees out of clay and used toothpicks to stick them to the mountain slopes. The detailed display featured several notecards with neatly hand-lettered titles and interesting facts about volcanoes.

On the day of the science fair, the girls saw each other's entries. Each girl admired the other's project. "I like your trees and rocks," Lea said to Bernadette.

"Thanks," Bernadette replied. "I can't wait to see your volcano in action!" They wished each other good luck and waited for the judges to choose the best project.

SKILL PRACTICE Read the item. Write your response.

1. Name two similar features of both girls' science projects.

2. What does Bernadette's project have that Lea's does *not* have?

3. What is the major difference between the girls' science projects?

STRATEGY PRACTICE Describe a project that you did for school or for a competition. Explain how your experience was similar to or different from the characters' experiences.

Compare and Contrast — WEEK 15, DAY 2

READ THE PASSAGE Think about how humans and ants are alike and different.

Complex Creatures

Humans are a complex species. We build structures to live in. We communicate with each other, which enables us to work in teams. We can adapt to most climates on Earth. We can eat almost any plant or animal, and we can grow our own food. These abilities set us apart from most species.

There is another type of creature, however, that can do all these things and more. In fact, these animals can also lift almost twenty times their own body weight. And their species has been on Earth for about 100 million years. You have probably seen their colonies in your backyard or neighborhood. They're ants!

Ants live on every continent except Antarctica. They use their antennae to communicate with one another, and they work together to build homes or to carry objects. Like humans, they also farm. Leafcutter ants farm fungus in their homes and use leaves as fertilizer. Other species of ants "raise" aphids, small insects that produce a special liquid. The ants take care of the aphids and keep them nearby so the ants can drink the liquid.

Of course, ants are also different from humans. Ants live mostly underground. Their colonies are made of complex tunnels in the dirt. And their life span is much shorter than ours. Individual ants typically live for only about three months, while humans can live for decades.

SKILL PRACTICE Read the item. Write your response.

1. How is the ants' behavior toward aphids similar to something humans do?
   _____
   _____

2. How do ants' homes differ from human homes?
   _____
   _____

3. What part of the text was easiest for you to visualize? Why?
   _____

STRATEGY PRACTICE List three interesting facts about ants that you learned from the passage.

_____
_____
_____

Make Inferences

WEEK 15 DAY 3

READ THE PASSAGE Use clues from the text and your own knowledge to make inferences about the competition for fossils.

Bone Wars

The idea of huge reptiles roaming the earth has fascinated people since the very first fossils were discovered. Interest in prehistoric creatures was at an all-time high during the late 1800s, and people who discovered fossils were practically considered celebrities. Two men in particular were in a big hurry to discover new specimens and become famous for their finds.

Othniel Marsh and Edward Cope were both scientists in the field of natural history, and the competition between them was bitter. It began when Marsh paid some of Cope's fossil diggers to send fossils to him. Cope worked quickly to report his findings so Marsh couldn't publish articles about a subject before Cope did. Working quickly to outdo each other, both men made mistakes on occasion. Cope discovered a species called *Elasmosaurus,* but he incorrectly placed the skull at the end of the tail when he displayed the skeleton. Marsh discovered an example of *Apatosaurus* but mistakenly gave it the skull of a completely different animal.

Despite their mistakes, the two men made many valuable discoveries. Between them, Cope and Marsh discovered dinosaur species including *Stegosaurus* and *Triceratops,* as well as other giant lizards such as the sail-backed *Dimetrodon* and the winged *Pteranodon.* Imagine what else the two men could have accomplished if they had worked together.

SKILL PRACTICE Read the item. Write your response.

1. What is the author's opinion of these two researchers? Cite text evidence in your response.

2. Draw two conclusions that apply to both *Elasmosaurus* and *Dimetrodon.*

3. How is the title appropriate for the text?

STRATEGY PRACTICE Describe a time when you were eager to finish something before someone else did. What happened?

Make Inferences — WEEK 15 DAY 4

READ THE PASSAGE Use clues from the text to make inferences about the Iroquois Confederacy.

The First American Democracy

You might assume that democracy first came to North America when the United States government was founded. But in fact, the first democratic body was a confederation of Native American tribes.

The Iroquois Confederacy, or Iroquois League, began sometime between 1570 and 1600, in what is now New York State. It included the Mohawk, Oneida, Onondaga, Cayuga, and Seneca tribes. Each tribe member had one vote to elect a chief. Each chief had one vote at the common council of tribes. If a group did not want to remain in the Confederacy, they could leave at any time. Also, any group was allowed to join the Confederacy as long as they agreed to the rules.

In 1722, the Tuscarora tribe joined the Confederacy, which then became known to European settlers as the Six Nations. However, the member tribes of the Six Nations called themselves *Haudenosaunee* (ho-dee-no-SHO-nee), which means "people building the longhouse." They considered their confederation to be like a big house in which all the tribes lived, helping and protecting one another.

During the American Revolution, the Six Nations were divided. Some tribes helped the American colonists, and some helped the British. After the Americans finally won the war against Britain and its allies in 1779, the members of the Confederacy all migrated to new homelands. In this way, the first democracy in America was split apart by the second democracy.

SKILL PRACTICE Read the item. Write your response.

1. *The Cayuga tribe was the most powerful one in the Iroquois Confederacy.* Cite text evidence to prove this statement true or false.

2. Explain why the tribes referred to themselves as *Haudenosaunee*.

3. How did the American Revolution cause problems for the Six Nations?

STRATEGY PRACTICE Describe something in the passage that you understood better after rereading it.

Compare and Contrast
Make Inferences
WEEK 15 DAY 5

READ THE PASSAGE Notice the different solutions that Gina, Julius, and Eddy have on moving day.

Moving Day

Gina, Julius, and Eddy sat on Uncle Tim's living room floor. Uncle Tim was moving across town, and the kids were trying to decide how to work together to pack their uncle's books.

"Julius, you can start putting the books into boxes," Gina directed.

"No," Julius argued. "I think Eddy should do that. I'm the strongest, so it's best if I carry the boxes to the truck after Eddy has packed them."

"I don't want to pack them," grumbled Eddy. "I want to watch TV."

"Too bad, Eddy," said Gina. "Your job is to put the books into the boxes. Then I'll tape the boxes shut, and Julius will carry them out."

"I have a better idea," Eddy declared.

"Eddy!" Gina and Julius both said as they stood up, annoyed with their brother. "We know you want to watch TV," Gina said, "but Uncle Tim needs your help today."

"I *know*!" Eddy responded. "I want to help. How about if you put the books into the boxes and I close the boxes—but not with tape?" Eddy then dragged a box of books to the center of the living room. He folded down the flaps on the top of the box in clockwise order and finished by tucking half of the last one under the first one. Then he tipped the box over on its side. The flaps stayed shut, and nothing fell out. "See?" Eddy exclaimed.

Gina crossed her arms and raised her eyebrows. "Fine. I guess I'll pack, then," she said.

Eddy smiled. He clicked the TV remote and waited for his sister to finish filling a box.

SKILL PRACTICE Read the item. Write your response.

1. Why should the strongest person carry the boxes to the moving truck?

   _____

   _____

2. Have the children come up with the most efficient way to help Uncle Tim? Defend your stance.

   _____

   _____

3. Why is Eddy smiling at the end of the text?

   _____

STRATEGY PRACTICE If you were helping someone move, which would you rather do—pack, tape shut, or carry boxes? Explain your answer to a partner.

Character and Setting — WEEK 16, DAY 1

READ THE PASSAGE Think about the subject of the biography and where the events take place.

The World's Greatest Athlete

On a late July day in 1912, the crowd in Stockholm, Sweden, went wild as Jim Thorpe emerged on the field. He had just won an Olympic gold medal in both the decathlon and the pentathlon. A decathlon is a group of ten track and field events. A pentathlon is made up of five events. That year, the pentathlon consisted of the long jump, javelin throw, discus throw, 200-meter dash, and 1500-meter run.

Jim Thorpe was born in 1888 near Prague, Oklahoma, on Sac-Fox tribal land. His Indian name was Wa-Tho-Huk, which means "Bright Path." The path would indeed be bright for the athlete, who became one of America's earliest sports heroes. On that day in 1912 when Thorpe won his gold medals, the King of Sweden told him, "Sir, you are the greatest athlete in the world."

After the Olympics, Thorpe played professional football, baseball, and basketball. Thorpe retired from sports in 1928, at age 41. In 1963, he was named to the Pro Football Hall of Fame.

In 1913, the Olympic Committee learned that Thorpe had been paid for playing baseball prior to the Olympics. This was against Olympic rules at the time, so they took away Thorpe's medals. The committee restored his medals in 1982. Today, the legend of Jim Thorpe lives on.

SKILL PRACTICE Read the item. Write your response.

1. Where and when did Jim Thorpe win the gold medals?

   _____
   _____

2. Name two adjectives that describe Thorpe. Explain your choices.

   _____
   _____

3. Describe the controversy that Thorpe had to face.

   _____
   _____

STRATEGY PRACTICE Choose three events mentioned in the passage. Write them in chronological order (the order in which they occurred in Jim's life). Include the years they happened.

_____
_____

Character and Setting — WEEK 16, DAY 2

READ THE PASSAGE Visualize the setting of the story as you read.

Climbing Half Dome

Pete's mouth dropped open when he first saw the mountain he was supposed to climb. The tall, gray granite mountain known as "Half Dome" looked like half of a giant hard-boiled egg. The mountain towered majestically over a river valley filled with evergreen trees. Half Dome was covered in snow that day, which would add to the difficulty and danger of climbing it.

"Let's go!" said Pete's friend Lisa, adjusting her backpack as she started along the trail.

Pete wondered if it was really safe to climb the face of the mountain. They had spent half an hour walking toward Half Dome. As they approached, the mountain seemed to stretch and disappear into the clouds. It was even larger up close than he had thought. "I'm not sure about this," Pete said, letting his fear show.

"Come on, don't worry!" Lisa called from a few paces ahead of him. "It won't be as scary as it looks." She smiled and waited for Pete to catch up.

Finally, at the mountain's base, Pete saw a thin but strong-looking cable stretching up the side of the rock. Climbers were using footholds—boards bolted into the granite—and holding on to the cable to pull themselves along. Lisa grabbed the cable and grinned. "Ready, Pete?" she asked.

The cable stretched hundreds of feet above him. "I can't wait!" Pete replied excitedly.

SKILL PRACTICE Read the item. Write your response.

1. What is the setting of this story?

2. Use text evidence to prove that Pete is scared of Half Dome.

3. Why does the author compare Half Dome to half a hard-boiled egg?

STRATEGY PRACTICE Draw a picture to show what Pete sees at the beginning of the story.

READ THE PASSAGE Think about the message, or theme, in this description of a famous landmark.

Alcatraz: From Prison to Preserve

Alcatraz Island was once home to many of America's toughest, most infamous criminals, including Al Capone and Robert "Birdman of Alcatraz" Stroud. Alcatraz was an island prison where no inmate ever successfully escaped, a chunk of land so remote and barren that it earned the nickname "The Rock." However, not all residents of Alcatraz Island arrived in handcuffs.

When Spanish explorers discovered the island in 1775, they called it *La Isla de los Alcatraces,* or "Island of the Pelicans." Pelicans weren't the only birds living on the island, but the name *Alcatraz* stuck.

Humans inhabited Alcatraz for the next two hundred years. This island was home to a lighthouse, a military fort, and, later, the maximum-security prison that made it famous. It was nearly impossible to escape from this jail located in the middle of San Francisco Bay.

In 1963, the prison was closed. But in 1973, Alcatraz became part of the Golden Gate National Recreation Area. Snowy egrets and black-crowned night herons are among the birds that make their homes on the island today. These birds, and small animals such as deer mice and salamanders, live where soldiers and prisoners once watched waves crash against the shore. While much of Alcatraz's fame comes from its history as a place of guards and locked cells, another part of the story comes from the island's wild, natural beauty.

SKILL PRACTICE Read the item. Write your response.

1. For what is the island of Alcatraz best known?

2. How does this text reflect on the theme of change?

3. What is the setting for this text? Include as many details as you can.

STRATEGY PRACTICE Did the author organize the passage mainly by sequence of events, by comparing two things, or by both? Explain your answer.

READ THE PASSAGE As you read, think about what the author wants to tell you about nature.

Desert Beauty

If you ask most people about the desert, they might describe sand and rocks and an occasional shrub. Arches National Park in Utah shows a different scene. Visitors to Arches are astonished by the life and color in the desert. Wildflowers and blooming cactuses are a bright contrast to the red rock. Deep-blue Steller's jays flit and hop, while red-tailed hawks soar overhead.

Of course, the park is most famous for its magnificent landforms. More than 2,000 natural arches have been discovered in the park. Some of these rock formations are free standing, forming graceful curves against cloudless skies. Others jut out from canyon walls and rocky cliffs.

These desert arches were created over the course of 100 million years, as wind and water slowly wore away the rock. Although the arches took millions of years to form, it takes only seconds to lose an arch forever. In 1991, Landscape Arch, the park's largest arch, lost a slab of rock 60 feet (18 m) long. The arch still stands, but it is now much more fragile. In 2008, the bridge of another famous arch, Wall Arch, collapsed completely. Located along a popular trail, the 71-foot (22-m) arch finally gave way to the forces of gravity and erosion.

In the beauty of this desert park, paved roads and cars are the only interruption to the natural scene. But these modern conveniences make it possible for people to enjoy nature's spectacular work while it still exists.

SKILL PRACTICE Read the item. Write your response.

1. Why does the author think that park visitors are surprised by what they see?

   _____
   _____

2. What makes the arches so fragile?

   _____
   _____

3. What sentence in the text tells what Arches National Park is best known for? Use quotation marks.

   _____
   _____

STRATEGY PRACTICE Underline words and phrases in the passage that helped you form a mental image of Arches National Park.

Character and Setting — WEEK 16
Theme — DAY 5

READ THE PASSAGE   Think about what the author wants you to know about Wall Street.

The Road to Wall Street

A Wall of Wood

In 1653, Dutch colonists inhabited the island of what is now Manhattan, New York. To protect their colony against invaders, the Dutch erected a wooden wall. It was tall and strong, but the wall was no match for the British, who took over the Dutch colony in 1664. The British destroyed the wall and paved the narrow path where the wall had once stood. They called it Wall Street.

Business Beginnings

Over the next 100 years, Wall Street became a popular place to do business. Trades and transactions frequently took place in coffeehouses. A group of merchants met regularly under a buttonwood tree in front of 68 Wall Street. In 1792, twenty-four of these businessmen signed the Buttonwood Agreement, forming what would eventually become the New York Stock Exchange.

Wall Street Today

Today, Wall Street is not only the center of American finance but one of the economic capitals of the world. Computers hum, phones ring, and large amounts of money trade hands every day in busy office buildings. Sidewalks bustle with bankers and stockbrokers whose decisions affect individuals, corporations, and even our nation's economy. Some people wonder whether the power and strength of Wall Street will last, or if it will fall just like the actual wall did.

SKILL PRACTICE   Read the item. Write your response.

1. What is the author's purpose for writing this text?

2. Describe Wall Street in 1653.

3. How are the people who work on Wall Street today like those who did so in 1792?

STRATEGY PRACTICE   Why does the passage have three parts? Describe the purpose of each part.

Author's Purpose — WEEK 17, DAY 1

READ THE PASSAGE As you read, think about why the author wrote the passage.

A Plastic Eye

Today, just about everyone has a camera. We can take pictures with our cellphones, e-mail photos to our friends, and print out pictures from a computer in a matter of seconds. Thirty years ago, however, cameras were not as simple to use or readily available. They used film, which was expensive and had to be processed with special chemicals in order to make prints. Then, in 1982, a new type of camera made photography easier and more affordable. It was a film camera, but it had a built-in flash and other conveniences. The camera was called the Holga.

The Holga camera was made completely of plastic. Even the lens, which is normally made from high-quality glass on most cameras, was plastic. Plastic is cheaper than metal or glass, so the camera makers could keep the Holga's price low enough for most people to afford.

However, once people began using the Holga, they noticed problems. Sometimes dark spots appeared at the corners of the photos. Sometimes the colors that appeared in the photos were different from the colors of the actual objects photographed. The camera's cheap construction and materials allowed light to leak inside the camera and affect the film.

Although some customers were upset about these defects, many people liked the strange and often unique effects that the camera produced. Professional photographers began using the camera to photograph landscapes, people, and street scenes. Even today, in a world filled with precision equipment, some people choose the unpredictable Holga to take unique pictures.

SKILL PRACTICE Read the item. Write your response.

1. What is the author's purpose for writing this text?

_____

_____

2. Why did the Holga quickly lose its popularity?

_____

_____

3. Why do some people still enjoy using the Holga?

_____

_____

STRATEGY PRACTICE Write a question that you would ask a photographer who uses a Holga camera.

_____

Author's Purpose — WEEK 17, DAY 2

READ THE PASSAGE Think about the author's purpose as you read about an unusual spice.

Red Threads

Few of us think twice about how much it costs to sprinkle a little spice on our food. But there is one spice—the most expensive one in the world—that can cost more than $1,000 per pound (0.45 kg). It has been used in kitchens, as well as in artwork and cosmetics, for thousands of years. The color of this spice is beautiful and unique. Buddhist monks use it as the official color of their prayer robes. What makes this spice, called *saffron,* so treasured?

Saffron comes from a small flower called a crocus. Each blossom grows three tiny red threads, or stigmas, which are then dried and sold as saffron threads. The dried threads can also be ground and sold as powder. It takes 75,000 crocus blossoms, or 225,000 stigmas, to produce one pound of dried saffron. That's a patch of flowers the size of a football field! In addition, the tiny stigmas must be picked by hand.

Saffron is prized for its rich color and powerful flavor, which some people compare to bitter honey. Just a pinch of the powdered spice is enough to flavor a pound of rice and give it a deep golden color. Even though crocus stigmas are red, the spice turns foods or liquids a golden yellow.

Throughout history, saffron has also been used as a medicine. According to modern studies, saffron may even lift a person's mood. This precious spice may come at a high price, but many people believe it is worth every penny.

SKILL PRACTICE Read the item. Write your response.

1. What is the author's purpose for the third paragraph?

2. For what two reasons is saffron so expensive?

3. Why does the author include the details about the size of the field and picking the blossoms by hand?

STRATEGY PRACTICE Describe a spice that you are familiar with. Explain one way that you use it.

Prediction — WEEK 17, DAY 3

READ THE PASSAGE Use your own knowledge and clues from the text to make predictions about the first dog in space.

The First Dog in Space

In October 1957, Russia launched the first man-made satellite, called *Sputnik*, into orbit. Russian scientists immediately began working on new experiments in space. They wanted to see if living things could exist in the weightlessness of space and survive outside Earth's atmosphere.

Russian scientists decided to use a dog to test the effects of space conditions. They collected several stray dogs from the streets of Moscow for the experiment. After a series of tests, one dog proved to be the best candidate. She was named Laika or "Little Curly." Americans called her "Muttnik"—the *Sputnik* mutt!

Laika blasted off aboard *Sputnik 2* on November 3, 1957. She survived the launch and orbited Earth four times, managing the weightlessness of space. Sadly, the spacecraft could not be brought back to Earth, and Laika died in space. This sparked discussion around the world about animal rights. Today, Laika is honored alongside the human cosmonauts of Russia's space program. A monument was placed at a research facility in Moscow in 2008. Although *Sputnik 2* was her one and only flight, Laika is remembered as a space pioneer.

SKILL PRACTICE Read the item. Write your response.

1. What did people learn from Laika's flight?

2. What is the greatest benefit of Laika's journey into space?

3. Predict the result of the animal rights discussion.

STRATEGY PRACTICE Write two questions that you have about Laika or *Sputnik*.

WEEK 17
Prediction
DAY 4

READ THE PASSAGE Use clues from the story to make predictions about the characters and their actions.

Lights, Action, Snakes!

"Cut!" the director yelled. "Excellent work, everyone! Take a break before the next scene."

Sam and Diane, the stars of the film, walked off the set together. Sam removed his wool cap and squeezed it nervously.

"You seem worried," Diane said.

"Snakes creep me out," whispered Sam, shuddering. "I hate being anywhere near them."

"The scene won't take long," Diane reassured him. "Just get it out of the way, and you won't have to think about it anymore."

"Why can't they use fake snakes? Or a stunt double—someone to play the scene for me?" Sam asked. "Or better yet, maybe *you* could hold the snakes!" he suggested.

Diane shook her head. "No, no. That wouldn't make sense in the movie."

"Well, it makes sense to me," replied Sam.

"Oh, come on," Diane said. "Think of your reputation. A big, strong action star like you— What would happen if your fans knew how scared you were of some harmless little reptiles?"

Sam narrowed his eyes. "You wouldn't dare tell."

"I would if you tried to get out of it," Diane threatened.

Sam paused for a moment. "You're right," he said. "I wouldn't want that."

SKILL PRACTICE Read the item. Write your response.

1. Why do you think Diane threatened Sam?

___

2. What will Sam probably do next?

___

3. Draw a conclusion about a type of movie in which Sam would refuse to play a role.

___

STRATEGY PRACTICE How would you feel if you had to act in a scene with snakes? Explain your answer.

___

Author's Purpose / Prediction — WEEK 17, DAY 5

READ THE PASSAGE Think about what might happen next, based on events in the story.

The Visitor

Herbie could barely stay in his seat. A jazz musician had come to speak to the class today, and Herbie had so many questions for him. The visitor was a short man with a wide-brimmed hat and a colorful suit. Herbie's teacher introduced the visitor as Terrence Harris, a clarinet player. "I'm sure the students will enjoy hearing about your music, Mr. Harris," she said.

"Please," said the man, "call me Terry."

Terry talked for a few minutes about music in general. Then he began talking about jazz, and his whole face lit up. He described what was unique about jazz music, and he explained how he had become a professional clarinet player. After a while, he asked the class if they had any questions. Herbie raised his hand.

"What's the best way to become a jazz musician?" Herbie asked.

Terry laughed. "First, find a musical instrument that lets you breathe music through it. Next, practice that instrument every day for the rest of your life."

Herbie's eyes opened wide. "I want to start practicing right now!" he shouted, jumping out of his chair.

"That's the spirit!" Terry said. "But why don't you wait until after school? Jazz players need to get good grades, too. When I was a young man, I didn't think much of school."

"Really? What do you mean?" Herbie asked as he settled in his seat again.

"Yes, really," Terry replied. "It all began when I was eleven years old. . ."

SKILL PRACTICE Read the item. Write your response.

1. What is the author's purpose for writing this text?

2. Why does the author state that Herbie could barely stay in his seat at the start of the text?

3. What will happen next? Explain.

STRATEGY PRACTICE What question would you ask Terry if you were in Herbie's class?

Nonfiction Text Features — WEEK 18, DAY 1

READ THE INFORMATION Think about which text features help you follow this interview.

David Cooper, Forensic Scientist

CareerWatch: As a forensic scientist, you help solve crimes. What's the scariest situation you have found yourself in while working on a case?

David: Actually, my job is very safe. I work right here in this lab. I analyze data and materials. I hardly ever visit the crime scene. In fact, the most dangerous part of my job is the chemicals I use to develop fingerprints.

CareerWatch: On television, forensic scientists are often shown at crime scenes or running after criminals. Are you saying your job isn't like that?

David: That's right. All the drama on TV is meant to make the shows more interesting. But the jobs of crime scene investigators and forensic scientists are very different. Investigators bring in all the evidence, and I work to piece it together in the crime lab.

CareerWatch: Tell us about some of the tools and materials you work with every day.

David: Our lab has different stations for different tasks. We have chemicals and machines that can analyze DNA, fingerprints, hair samples, and other evidence. Today, I'm putting together a complete fingerprint from a smudged sample that the investigators found at the crime scene.

CareerWatch: On TV shows, forensic scientists use fancy computer equipment such as facial recognition software, 3-D displays of crime scenes, and giant computer screens. Is that an accurate depiction?

David: Well, we do have high-tech equipment, but it's not exactly as you see on TV. Studying evidence isn't nearly as quick and easy as Hollywood makes it seem.

SKILL PRACTICE Read the item. Write your response.

1. What would be a better title for this text? Explain.

2. Where does this interview take place? How do you know?

3. Where would this interview most likely be published? Why?

STRATEGY PRACTICE Give one example of how forensic science is different from the way it is shown on TV.

Nonfiction Text Features — WEEK 18, DAY 2

READ THE INFORMATION Study the content and organization of this book about movies.

Contents

Introduction	i
Silent Films	1
The Sounds of Progress	17
A Colorful World	33
Hollywood Rises Again	47
Big-Budget Blockbusters	55
Low-Budget Thrillers	67
Special Effects	71
Filmmaking Today	81
What Will Tomorrow Bring?	89
Conclusion	97
Index	100

By the 1930s, millions of Americans were flocking to movie theaters. New technology and big budgets brought major changes to filmmaking. It is no wonder that Hollywood and the actors who worked there gained enormous fame.

In 1939, *The Wizard of Oz* turned heads with its huge budget and cast. A young actress named Judy Garland sang the opening notes of "Over the Rainbow" and launched herself into the spotlight.

At a time when movies were still filmed mainly in black and white, Hollywood stars had to shine brightly enough to keep audiences interested. *Casablanca* opened in 1942 and featured a charming Humphrey Bogart and a beautiful Ingrid Bergman. These Hollywood stars proved that they didn't need elaborate makeup or flashy special effects to entertain a nation. They needed only the spotlight and an audience to love them.

SKILL PRACTICE Read the item. Write your response.

1. In which chapter would the excerpt on the right appear? Use text evidence to tell how you know.

2. To which page would you turn to start reading about the future of filmmaking? How can you tell?

3. What did Judy Garland and Ingrid Bergman have in common?

STRATEGY PRACTICE What clues in the chapter titles and the excerpt suggest that this book is organized in chronological order?

READ THE PASSAGE — Use the illustration to help you visualize a natural geyser.

Yellowstone's Faithful Fountain

Old Faithful is a natural geyser, an eruption of hot water and steam into the air. Underground hot springs and water pressure work together to create this natural wonder, which has fascinated visitors of Yellowstone Park for more than 100 years.

One thing that makes Old Faithful special is how regularly it erupts. The geyser puts on a show about every 75 minutes, an event that gave the geyser its name and claim to fame.

Visitors to Yellowstone National Park can watch Old Faithful seven days a week during daylight hours, but they must be careful to keep their distance. The geyser shoots more than 3,700 gallons (14,006 L) of boiling water over 100 feet (31 m) into the air!

SKILL PRACTICE — Read the item. Write your response.

1. Where might you find this text?

2. What might happen if a tourist got too close to Old Faithful?

3. What makes Old Faithful different from most other geysers?

STRATEGY PRACTICE — Describe the most important details shown in the illustration.

Visual Information — WEEK 18, DAY 4

READ THE CHART Notice how the information in the temperature chart is arranged.

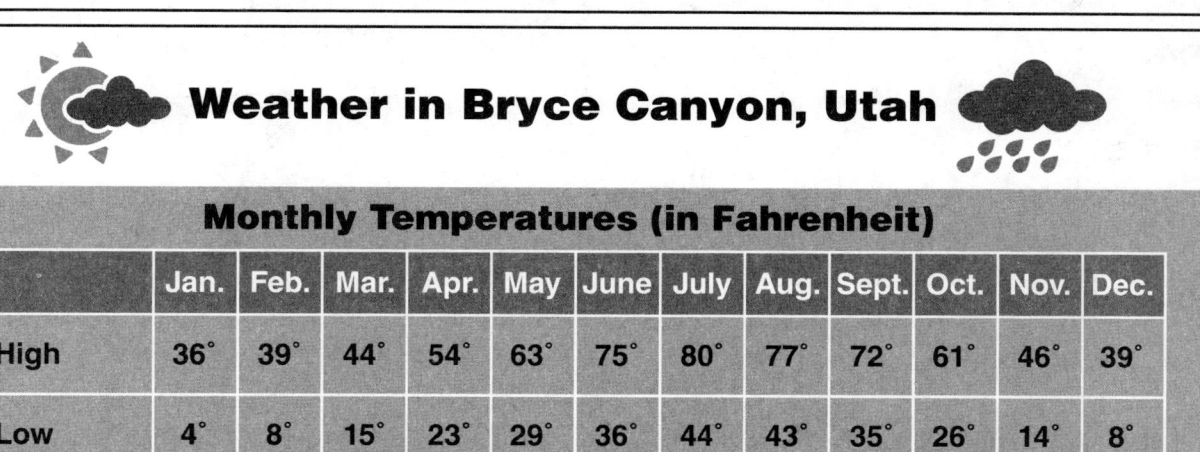

Weather in Bryce Canyon, Utah

Monthly Temperatures (in Fahrenheit)

	Jan.	Feb.	Mar.	Apr.	May	June	July	Aug.	Sept.	Oct.	Nov.	Dec.
High	36°	39°	44°	54°	63°	75°	80°	77°	72°	61°	46°	39°
Low	4°	8°	15°	23°	29°	36°	44°	43°	35°	26°	14°	8°
Average	20°	23°	29°	38°	46°	55°	62°	60°	53°	43°	30°	23°

SKILL PRACTICE Read the item. Write your response.

1. A person is planning a trip to Bryce Canyon. How should she use this chart?

2. During which month does Bryce Canyon experience the coldest temperatures? How can you tell?

3. Which two months have the same average temperature? How do you know?

STRATEGY PRACTICE Explain why the information in the chart is organized in columns and rows. How does this organization help you see and understand the information?

Nonfiction Text Features — Visual Information
WEEK 18 DAY 5

READ THE INFORMATION Study the index and the excerpt from this illustrated book on China.

Index

(A–N)

art, **21–23**
Beijing, **52, 67**
Chinese calendar, **18–19**
economy, **23–40**
emperors, Ming, **16–20**
  see also *Hongwu* and *Yongle*
Forbidden City, **11, 67–68**
Grand Canal, **60–63**
Great Wall, **45–50**
Hongwu period, **33–51**
maps, **55, 148**
Nanjing, **52, 67**
paper money, **24**
philosophy, **45–50**

(R–Z)

religion
  Buddhism, **78–81**
  Chinese folk, **75–78**
  Taoism, **81–83**
silk, **17, 23**
society
  customs, **131–135**
  jobs, **121, 145–147**
  social classes, **53–57, 120, 131**
trade, **60, 72, 121, 130**
warfare
  civil war, **167–169**
  with Japan, **174–180**
  with Mongolia, **180–183**
Yongle period, **52–69**
Zheng He, **55, 148–151**
zoo, **57**

Emperor Yongle (yoong-LAW) was one of the most powerful emperors in the Ming dynasty. He ruled for 22 years and made many cultural advances. One of his achievements was the construction of the Forbidden City.

SKILL PRACTICE Read the item. Write your response.

1. In which page ranges would you expect to see the illustration on the right? Explain.

___

2. Which pages contain information about the war China fought against Japan?

___

3. To which page would you turn to start reading about the religion known as Taoism?

___

STRATEGY PRACTICE What important information can you learn about the Ming dynasty from the illustration and its caption?

___

Main Idea and Details — **WEEK 19 DAY 1**

READ THE PASSAGE Pause after each paragraph and think about the main idea.

Life on a Sheep Farm

Life on Ernest Wilkins's sheep farm in southern Australia is not easy, but the work is satisfying. Sheep farming is hard physical work, and it requires a caring attitude toward animals.

On a typical day, Wilkins awakens at sunrise and eats a hearty breakfast to give him energy for the long hours ahead. Wilkins's first stop is the shed where all the mother sheep and their young lambs live. He fills the water trough and feeds the mother sheep a special blend of cornmeal and nutrients. He gives the lambs a different food blend. Next, Wilkins goes to a second shed to feed the other adult sheep, which eat a diet of plain hay. He spends the rest of the morning making repairs around the farm. He mends fences, fixes farm machinery, and performs regular maintenance on his truck.

Shearing season is the busiest time on the farm, and it occurs once a year. To shear the sheep, Wilkins and his sons move the fluffy sheep into the shearing shed. They work together to carefully shave the fleece, or wool, from each sheep. Then they collect, sort, and process the fleece to remove any twigs, burrs, or other materials stuck in it. On market days, Wilkins and his sons bring bales of raw fleece into town to sell or to trade for supplies needed for the farm.

A few sheep on the farm produce milk. Wilkins milks these sheep and processes the milk. He then sells the milk to other farmers, who use it to make cheese and yogurt. Running a sheep farm is a lot of work, but Wilkins enjoys it. He can't imagine any job he'd rather be doing.

SKILL PRACTICE Read the item. Write your response.

1. Which sentence in the text states the main idea? Use quotation marks.

2. What products are produced on Ernest Wilkins's farm?

3. Write the main idea of the third paragraph in your own words.

STRATEGY PRACTICE Explain how the details in paragraph 2 support the main idea of the entire passage.

Main Idea and Details — WEEK 19, DAY 2

READ THE PASSAGE Look for details that support the main ideas about rongorongo.

Rongorongo

Easter Island, located in the Pacific Ocean about 2,000 miles (3,219 km) west of Chile, is famous for its large human-shaped statues called *moai* (MOH-eye). These statues have fascinated people for many years. But the moai are not the only interesting thing about Easter Island.

Rongorongo is an old system of writing that was developed on Easter Island. Scholars believe that it was invented without the influence of other written languages. The symbols that make up rongorongo include picture symbols—animals, birds, plants, and people—and geometric shapes, such as triangles and diamonds, that probably represented sounds. The island's inhabitants used sharp rocks or sharks' teeth to carve the symbols into stone or pieces of wood. Most likely, the only people who used rongorongo were royalty and religious leaders. Few other people on the island would have known how to read or write.

By the 18th century, the early culture of Easter Island was almost completely destroyed, and an understanding of rongorongo was lost. This has made studying the system of symbols like breaking a code. What makes it even more difficult is that fewer than 30 stone or wood objects with rongorongo carvings exist in the world.

Today, Spanish is the main language of Easter Island. Many people also learn Rapa Nui, a Polynesian language. But the mysterious writing system of rongorongo has faded into the past.

SKILL PRACTICE Read the item. Write your response.

1. What is the main idea of this text?

___

2. What makes rongorongo like a secret code?

___

3. Draw a conclusion about who destroyed the early culture of Easter Island.

___

STRATEGY PRACTICE Underline words or phrases in the passage that helped you form a mental image of rongorongo. Draw a picture to show what you visualized.

Sequence — Week 19, Day 3

READ THE PASSAGE Pay attention to the dates and events in Arizona's history.

The Grand Canyon State

On February 14, 1912, Arizona became the 48th state in the nation—the final territory of the U.S. mainland to join the union. The history of humans living in the region, however, stretches back many thousands of years. The land that became Arizona was home to prehistoric peoples as far back as 10,000 BC. There is evidence that people were farming the land more than 4,000 years ago. Around AD 1200, an extreme drought caused populations to decline, and some civilizations, including the Anasazi and Hohokam, disappeared.

One of the first Europeans to explore the region was the Spanish adventurer Francisco Vásquez de Coronado. He arrived around 1540. Members of his expedition were among the first Europeans to explore the Grand Canyon, which would eventually attract tourists to Arizona.

In 1821, Mexico gained its independence from Spain and claimed the land that became Arizona. Just two decades later, though, Mexico gave up the land when it lost the U.S.-Mexican War. Then in 1853, the United States bought northern Arizona and New Mexico in a deal called the Gadsden Purchase. The California Gold Rush, which began in 1849, brought people from the eastern United States to the West. Many of these people settled in Arizona.

By 1863, Arizona had become an official U.S. territory. By 1910, just two years before Arizona became a state, its population had reached more than 204,000. As of 2009, nearly 6.6 million people were living in "The Grand Canyon State."

SKILL PRACTICE Read the item. Write your response.

1. In the Gadsden Purchase, who did the United States pay and what did the nation buy?

2. Reread the first paragraph. Was Arizona the last state to join the United States? How can you tell?

3. What are the names of the Native American tribes that left the area more than 800 years ago?

STRATEGY PRACTICE Look back at the dates. Summarize the events in Arizona's history from 1821 to 1912.

WEEK 19 DAY 4 — Sequence

READ THE PASSAGE Pay attention to the events related to the publication of Peter Wright's book.

A Dangerous Book

In 1985, a retired British government employee named Peter Wright tried to publish a book about his life. But as soon as the British government heard about it, officials tried to prevent the book from being sold in England. The government even made it illegal for newspapers to print anything about the book. How could a book about a retired man's life be so dangerous?

Peter Wright had led an interesting life. He had been an officer with MI5, one of the British government's secret service agencies. Wright's book contained stories about people and events that MI5 didn't want anyone to know about. The government's attempt to ban the book, though, only drew attention to it. People wanted to know what all the fuss was about.

Although Wright's book, called *Spycatcher,* was not allowed in England, it was already available in other parts of the world. Some people bought the book outside the country and sneaked it in. The fact that this was illegal didn't stop the book from becoming popular.

British courts tried to prevent *Spycatcher* from being published in Australia, but they were unsuccessful. The book was published there in 1987. The following year, British law finally allowed people in England to own and sell the book.

Even after *Spycatcher* was published in England, the British government tried to prevent newspapers from reporting on it. The European Court of Human Rights fought back. In 1991, the British government lost its legal battle. It was a victory for newspaper publishers.

SKILL PRACTICE Read the item. Write your response.

1. Why was the British government so upset about Peter Wright's autobiography?

2. When did the British government first allow *Spycatcher* to be sold in England? Cite text evidence in your response.

3. What occurred when the British government tried to prevent the newspapers from reporting about the book?

STRATEGY PRACTICE Make a timeline showing the major events described in the passage.

Main Idea and Details — **WEEK 19**
Sequence — **DAY 5**

READ THE PASSAGE — Pay attention to the sequence of steps in the science experiment, and notice the details that tell you what happens in the story.

In the Lab

Roger mixed the blue liquid into the yellow liquid for the fifth time that day. The four previous attempts had failed. Each time, the experiment had produced only hydrogen. Quentin, a fellow scientist, had checked the calculations three times.

"OK, it turned green," Roger declared. "We've got that part right. What's step four?"

"Add 1 gram of aluminum powder," said Quentin.

Roger measured 1 gram of the silvery white powder and mixed it in. "OK, next?"

"Heat the mixture over a medium flame for 90 seconds," Quentin said.

Roger held the container over the flame with a pair of tongs. He looked at the second hand on his watch and counted 90 seconds.

"Now add the sulfur tablet and put in the stopper and tube," said Quentin.

Roger dropped a yellow disk into the container. The liquid inside fizzed and bubbled. He pushed a stopper into the neck of the container and slid a plastic tube into a hole in the center of the stopper. Quentin handed an instrument to Roger, who held it at the open end of the plastic tube, measuring the gas coming out. The two men stared at the instrument for 60 seconds.

"Just hydrogen," Roger sighed. Quentin's head drooped. "I hope the sixth time's a charm."

SKILL PRACTICE — Read the item. Write your response.

1. Which attempt of the experiment is described? Cite text evidence in your response.

_____

_____

2. What is the sixth step of the experiment?

_____

3. What does Roger do right after he adds the aluminum powder?

_____

_____

STRATEGY PRACTICE — Write the step in the experiment that was easiest for you to understand. Then write the step that was most difficult to understand.

_____

_____

Cause and Effect — WEEK 20, DAY 1

READ THE PASSAGE Look for causes and effects that explain what happens in the dance class.

The Never-Ending Lesson

The first 20 minutes of dance class always seemed to last forever. Melissa and Jane faced the mirrored wall, each with one arm curved overhead. Their arched and pointed feet in pink ballet shoes traced half-circles on the wood floor.

When the warm-up ended, the two girls collapsed, groaning. "My feet!" Jane moaned. "They're killing me!"

Mrs. Lark, their teacher, was not amused. "Stand up, girls," she insisted. "You need to be ready for the dance competition next month, and your turns need work."

Jane rubbed her sore feet. "We've been practicing all week," she complained.

The dance teacher clapped her hands sternly. "I won't let the two of you get lazy this time," she said. "Remember what happened last year?"

The two girls looked down in silence. They were remembering the judges and the crowd at last year's competition. It had been a huge disappointment.

"We should get back to work," Melissa mumbled, as she heaved herself up.

Jane was getting up, too. She tugged at her tights and pushed back her bangs. "We'll be ready," she assured Mrs. Lark as she positioned herself for turns, "even if we have to put in extra practice every day for the next four weeks."

"It'll be worth it," Melissa agreed. "Let's take it from the top."

SKILL PRACTICE Read the item. Write your response.

1. Why do the girls collapse at the start of the story?

_____
_____

2. What happened at last year's dance competition, and how do the girls feel about it?

_____

3. Why does Mrs. Lark clap?

_____
_____

STRATEGY PRACTICE Summarize what happens to Melissa and Jane in the story.

_____
_____

Cause and Effect — WEEK 20, DAY 2

READ THE PASSAGE Notice cause-and-effect relationships as you read about Nigerian music.

Nigerian Rhythms

The West African country of Nigeria is home to more than 250 different ethnic groups, each with its own culture. The region was a British colony until the mid-1900s, and modern Nigeria shows the influence of Britain. It has also been influenced by the United States and the Caribbean. Nigerian popular music combines traditional sounds with the sounds of jazz, reggae, rock-and-roll, gospel, and other imported music. The result is a unique mix of musical styles.

Traditional Nigerian music uses percussion instruments such as drums, gourd rattles, xylophones, and bells. These instruments produce strong beats, and Nigerian music is highly rhythmic. In fact, it often features two or more beat patterns played at the same time.

Traditional Nigerian music also includes wind instruments such as horns, trumpets, flutes, and whistles, as well as stringed instruments. The most common traditional stringed instrument is the musical bow. It looks like an arched piece of wood with a single string stretched across the two ends. The musician produces sounds by plucking the string or pushing an object across the string. However, modern Nigerian music is more likely to feature electric guitars.

In the 1980s, well-known Nigerian musicians recorded their music for international music producers. That's when Americans first became familiar with Nigerian pop. The catchy tunes and driving rhythms of this music were a huge hit!

SKILL PRACTICE Read the item. Write your response.

1. How did the United States and Caribbean cultures contribute to Nigerian pop music?

___

2. How was the world introduced to Nigerian pop music?

___

3. How does a musician produce sounds on the musical instrument known as a bow?

___

STRATEGY PRACTICE Write a question that you had about Nigerian music. Write the answer, too, if the passage provides the information.

___

© Evan-Moor Corp. • EMC 6365 • Daily Reading Comprehension

Fact and Opinion — WEEK 20, DAY 3

READ THE PASSAGE Identify the facts and opinions that the author gives about vampire bats.

Real-Life Vampires

When you hear about vampire bats, do you imagine dangerous, bloodsucking creatures? Does the thought of thousands of vampire bats in the night sky send you scurrying indoors? Vampire bats may seem creepy, but these small mammals aren't as terrifying as their name suggests. In fact, not only are they harmless to humans, but they can even help humans live longer.

You may be surprised to hear that vampire bats don't actually suck blood. Instead, they prick an animal with their two front teeth and lick the blood from the cut. A chemical in the bat's saliva prevents blood from clotting as it flows out. This allows the bat to feed without causing pain to its victim or even waking it up. The vampire bat takes only about two tablespoons (30 mL) of blood at a time.

Besides being mostly harmless, vampire bats are sweet, gentle creatures that live together in groups called *colonies*. Adult bats often adopt and care for orphaned bats. Like good neighbors, vampire bats are willing to share their nightly meals with each other during hard times. It seems that these gentle creatures live for the good of the colony.

How can humans benefit from these fascinating creatures? Scientists have studied ways to use the chemical in vampire bat saliva to break up blood clots in people who have had a stroke or a heart attack. The very same bats that inspire fear could actually help save human lives. It's just another reason that scientists are interested in these furry flying creatures.

SKILL PRACTICE Read the item. Write your response.

1. How might vampire bats help save people's lives?

_____
_____

2. Are there any opinions stated in the second paragraph? Explain.

_____
_____

3. What words in the third paragraph indicate the author's opinion about vampire bats?

_____
_____

STRATEGY PRACTICE Underline each sentence and phrase in the passage that helped you understand why people should not be afraid of vampire bats.

Fact and Opinion — WEEK 20, DAY 4

READ THE PASSAGE Think about which details are facts and which are opinions.

The Writer at the End of the Universe

Douglas Adams was a British writer who breathed new life into science fiction. Unlike other science fiction authors of his time, he didn't write about Martian invasions or flying saucers. His stories often included space travel, but his humor put a fresh spin on the galaxy.

Douglas Adams is best known for writing a series of books that began as a radio play. The first novel, called *The Hitchhiker's Guide to the Galaxy,* was published in 1979. In the series, Adams created a universe filled with funny and original characters, such as Marvin, a brilliant but depressed robot, and monsters that write bad poetry. Arthur Dent, the central character, is an unlikely hero who travels across the universe and has silly adventures. Readers who like to imagine new worlds and enjoy humorous writing should read the series.

Besides the *Hitchhiker's Guide* series, Adams also wrote many other wonderful books, television programs, and computer games. Although Adams died in 2001, millions of fans will remember him through his works. "I seldom end up where I wanted to go," Adams said, "but almost always end up where I need to be."

SKILL PRACTICE Read the item. Write your response.

1. Are there any facts stated in the first paragraph? Explain.

2. Are there any opinions stated in the last paragraph? Explain.

3. How does *The Hitchhiker's Guide to the Galaxy* compare to the types of books you like to read?

STRATEGY PRACTICE Write a question that you had about Adams or his books. Write the answer, too, if the passage provides that information.

Cause and Effect • Fact and Opinion — WEEK 20, DAY 5

READ THE PASSAGE Think about what happened to silent pictures and why. Notice which statements are facts and which are opinions.

The Golden Age of Silent Pictures

When people go to the movies today, they can settle in to watch and listen to a story. But what if when the lights dimmed and the movie began, there was no dialogue, sound effects, or music? That's what the first movies were like. Those silent films are important to film history.

When movie theaters showed silent films, a musician was often there to play live music along with the movie. Music was chosen to fit the mood of the movie. Occasionally, musicians or theater staff also produced sound effects, such as tires screeching or doors slamming. However, there was no sound in the movie itself. Instead, the story was told through the actors' motions and through words shown on the screen.

When movies first included sound, audiences weren't sure what to think. Not everyone was excited about the new type of film, which became known as the "talkie." Many silent film performers had trouble with the new format. Clara Bow, who was a famous silent-movie actress in the early 1920s, was too nervous about her voice to become a star in the world of talking pictures. She faded from the spotlight and left show business altogether.

The first movie with sound, *The Jazz Singer,* was released in 1927. It marked the beginning of a new era, although silent movies continued to be released for two more years. Talking pictures became a huge success, and Hollywood abandoned silent films.

SKILL PRACTICE Read the item. Write your response.

1. *The Great Train Robbery* is a silent movie produced in 1903. How did the audience follow its storyline?

2. What caused Clara Bow to leave show business?

3. *Silent films are an important part of movie history.* Write a short response that defends or opposes this statement.

STRATEGY PRACTICE In your own words, summarize what the passage is about.

Compare and Contrast — WEEK 21, DAY 1

READ THE PASSAGE Look for similarities and differences between Trina and Mark.

A Very Busy Day

December 26, the day after Christmas, was the busiest day of the year at the department store where Trina worked. Many people came to return or exchange gifts. Others came for the chance to buy things on sale. The store was so crowded that there was barely room to move.

Every store employee had to work that day. To handle the rush of customers, the store opened at 6 AM instead of 10 AM. Trina took her usual place at the returns counter. When it was time for her break, she headed to the employee cafeteria for a quick snack.

"It's crazy out there!" Trina said to Mark, a friend and fellow employee, who was slumped down in an armchair in the break room.

"Tell me about it," Mark groaned. "All five cash registers are going nonstop. I'm not sure I'm going to make it till closing time."

"Sure you will," Trina said cheerfully. "It's your first time, but this is my third year. I love working on the day after Christmas because the time goes by quickly. Also, if you stay positive, it makes the customers happier."

"I'm just not used to coming to work this early," Mark said. "I'm worn out."

"Let's see if we can switch places for a while," Trina suggested. "I'll take your cash register, and you take returns. Maybe a change of pace will help you out."

"Good idea," Mark perked up. "Thanks! I owe you one."

SKILL PRACTICE Read the item. Write your response.

1. How are Trina and Mark similar?

_____

_____

2. How are Trina and Mark different?

_____

_____

3. Explain why all the store employees are required to work on December 26.

_____

STRATEGY PRACTICE Describe a time you spent in a crowded place like this department store.

_____

_____

Compare and Contrast — WEEK 21, DAY 2

READ THE PASSAGE Think about how ice fishing can be compared to regular fishing.

Ice Fishing

Winter brings more than snow and cold weather to the northern United States. If the temperature dips low enough, the water in ponds and lakes begins to freeze on the surface. A thick enough layer of ice creates the right conditions for ice fishing.

This popular winter sport is similar in many ways to regular fishing. Both sports require lures—small dangling objects that look like food to a fish—and hooks attached to a line. And just like regular fishing, ice fishing requires skill and patience. It also provides an opportunity to socialize with friends or to enjoy quiet time by yourself.

However, ice fishing involves more work and equipment than regular fishing. To fish in unfrozen water, you simply need a rod, bait, and a good place to sit or stand near the water. Ice fishing, on the other hand, must be done on a layer of ice at least four inches (10 cm) thick—thick enough to support a great deal of weight. Ice fishers use a drill-like tool called an auger to make a hole about eight inches (20 cm) wide through the ice. Then they use a skimmer, a tool that looks like a large ladle with holes in it, to scoop out pieces of ice and to keep the hole clear.

Ice fishers also need special outerwear, including a thick winter coat, a hat, and gloves. Many ice fishers build shelters to protect themselves from the cold. Some shelters even have portable heaters and satellite TVs. After all, ice fishers want to stay comfortable while having fun!

SKILL PRACTICE Read the item. Write your response.

1. Name three similarities between fishing and ice fishing.

   _____

   _____

2. Name three differences between fishing and ice fishing.

   _____

   _____

3. Why does the ice have to be a specific thickness for ice fishers to set up?

   _____

   _____

STRATEGY PRACTICE Make a chart that lists the main features of ice fishing and regular fishing.

Make Inferences — WEEK 21, DAY 3

READ THE PASSAGE Make inferences about sleep paralysis, using clues from the text and your own experience.

Asleep or Awake?

Have you ever awakened and felt like you couldn't move? If so, it probably scared you. You may have thought something terrible had happened to you. Actually, many people have this experience on a regular basis. It is called *sleep paralysis*. Although it sounds scary, it is normal.

Sleep paralysis happens when a person is falling asleep or waking up. As the person falls asleep, his or her body slowly relaxes. Usually the person's mind relaxes at the same time, but occasionally the mind stays awake longer than the body. As a result, the person can be conscious, or aware, but have trouble moving or speaking. Sleep paralysis can also occur as you wake up. Fortunately, the condition rarely lasts for more than a few seconds. Movement and speech soon return to normal.

Some people report unusual experiences during sleep paralysis. They may hear, see, or feel things that don't exist. At one time, people thought that ghosts or monsters had entered the room and were holding them down, keeping them from moving. Science has helped us understand that such visions are actually part of sleep paralysis. Now we know that getting too little sleep, taking certain medications, and changing your sleep schedule can cause sleep paralysis. This condition can be scary if it happens to you, but it's just a trick that your mind is playing on your body.

SKILL PRACTICE Read the item. Write your response.

1. Carmen has slept for four hours when her alarm rings. As she awakens, she experiences sleep paralysis. Why?

   _____

   _____

2. Carmen tells you that her experience with sleep paralysis was frightening. What do you tell her?

   _____

3. Name the three underlying reasons for sleep paralysis.

   _____

   _____

STRATEGY PRACTICE How would you feel if you experienced sleep paralysis? What would you tell yourself, now that you have learned about this condition?

_____

_____

WEEK 21 DAY 4

Make Inferences

READ THE PASSAGE Make inferences about Sidney Poitier, using clues from the text and what you know about overcoming prejudice.

Sir Sidney Poitier

Sidney Poitier was born in 1927 and grew up on Cat Island in the Bahamas, which was a British colony at the time. His father was a poor farmer. Poitier moved to New York as a teenager and took a job as a dishwasher. Then he worked as a theater janitor in exchange for acting lessons. He began performing in plays and got his first Broadway role in 1946, in an all-black production of the Greek comedy *Lysistrata* (lis-uh-STRAH-tuh). His first movie role was in the 1950 film *No Way Out,* in which he played a black doctor who treats two white prisoners.

Tension between whites and blacks was a fact of life during the 1950s and 1960s. Poitier chose to play many roles that explored issues of race. In the 1967 movie *In the Heat of the Night,* for example, he played Virgil Tibbs, a detective from Philadelphia who investigates a murder in a small town in Mississippi. Tibbs and many of the characters that Poitier portrayed overcame prejudice and won the respect of others. Through his roles and his performances, Poitier helped create serious roles for African American actors and change people's views toward blacks.

During his career, Sidney Poitier directed nine movies and acted in more than 40. He has won many awards and has been nominated for even more. In 1963, he received an Oscar for his role in *Lilies of the Field*. This made him the first black actor to win an Academy Award for best actor. In 1974, Queen Elizabeth II of England "knighted" him, giving him the title "Sir Sidney Poitier." As a pioneer in the film industry, Sir Sidney continues to inspire many people today.

SKILL PRACTICE Read the item. Write your response.

1. Why do people consider Sidney Poitier inspirational?

___

2. Beginning in his teenage years, what was Poitier's goal? Cite text evidence to support your response.

___

3. How did Poitier's accomplishments help other African American actors and actresses?

___

STRATEGY PRACTICE Explain how social issues of the time influenced Sidney Poitier's career.

___

Compare and Contrast — WEEK 21
Make Inferences — DAY 5

READ THE PASSAGE Look for comparisons in Anil's life, and use clues from the text to make inferences about his decisions.

The Fish Thief: A Folk Tale from India

Anil and other men had been fishing in the stream since daybreak. Yet no one had caught a single fish. As daylight faded, Anil thought to himself, "These others may be honest fishermen, but I am not. I will go where I can find fish and take them, even if they aren't mine to take." So he packed up his fishing net and awaited the darkness.

Now, in this part of India, many large estates had lush gardens and beautiful lakes. The wealthy owners often left their gates open during the day so visitors could enjoy the lovely gardens. Occasionally, a wandering yogi, or holy man, would enter an estate and meditate there for weeks. Nobody seemed to mind. At night, the owners closed the gates securely.

Anil knew of a nearby estate with a lake full of fish, so he headed off in that direction. He climbed the wall and cast his net into the lake. The noise awakened the owner's servants, who began to search for the intruder. Hearing them, Anil disguised himself as a holy man and pretended to meditate. When the servants found him, they thought he was just a wise old yogi.

The next day, word spread that a great yogi was meditating beneath a tree on the estate. People began to bring fruits and other offerings, which they placed at Anil's feet. Some people even left coins. "This is strange," thought Anil. "I'm only pretending to be a holy man. But this life is much better than the life of a fish thief." From that moment on, Anil decided to become a real seeker of truth, and he spent the rest of his life in peaceful contemplation.

SKILL PRACTICE Read the item. Write your response.

1. How is Anil different from the other fishermen?

2. Why does Anil disguise himself? Does the disguise work?

3. How does Anil's goal change from the start of the story to the end?

STRATEGY PRACTICE Tell how this folk tale is like another story you know.

Character and Setting — WEEK 22, DAY 1

READ THE PASSAGE Think about the characters in the story and where the events take place.

Breathless

Alfred had been pestering Michael for weeks to go mountain biking with him in Boulder Park. Finally, Michael reluctantly agreed, but only after Alfred promised to help him study for a science test later in the week.

The whole way to the park, Michael felt grumpy. As they pedaled onto the dirt trail that snaked up the side of the rocky hill, he wondered if he should have stayed home and studied. Alfred knew what Michael was thinking, and he tried to reassure him. "It'll be fun, I promise. Besides, fresh air and exercise will be good for you."

"It's just a big dry mountain," Michael said. "I can't see how this will help me."

Alfred ignored Michael's complaints. "Look at that huge lizard!" he said, pointing to a scaly reptile sunbathing near a patch of cholla (CHOI-yuh) cactus.

"I've seen bigger," Michael said, panting as he struggled to keep up. His tires crunched along the steep, sandy path.

Before long, the two boys came around a bend. Alfred was grinning from ear to ear. "What are you smiling about?" Michael asked breathlessly. Then he saw what Alfred was looking at. A clear view of the city stretched to the east. Rugged mountains rose in the west.

"Now do you understand why I wanted you to come here?" Alfred asked.

Michael nodded, speechless, as he took in the spectacular view.

SKILL PRACTICE Read the item. Write your response.

1. Describe the setting of this text.

2. Which boy is more interested in nature? How can you tell?

3. Name two adjectives that describe Michael at the start of the story.

STRATEGY PRACTICE How does Michael's attitude change from the beginning of the story to the end?

Character and Setting — WEEK 22, DAY 2

READ THE PASSAGE Visualize the people and places in this passage about chariot racing.

Racing, Roman-Style

In ancient times, team sports were just as popular as they are today. One of the sports that drew huge crowds in ancient Rome was chariot racing. Fans cheered and shouted as horses pulled two-wheeled vehicles around long oval tracks to the finish line. The chariot drivers competed on teams and even wore team colors.

Circus Maximus, the largest racetrack in Rome, was more than 2,000 feet (610 m) long and 600 feet (183 m) wide. The arena had benches that surrounded the oval track on three sides and could seat 250,000 people. That's more than any American football stadium!

Many chariot drivers were slaves, but successful drivers could buy their freedom. Famous chariot drivers were respected nearly as much as emperors and senators. The best drivers were also nearly as wealthy. They were celebrated in statues and other works of art.

Chariot racing was a dangerous sport, though. Chariots could easily overturn, and drivers could be trampled to death. Also, the drivers could get tangled up in their own reins, which they wrapped around their bodies for control during the race.

Not everyone loved the races. Pliny the Younger, a famous ancient Roman author, wrote that he didn't understand why so many people wanted to watch horses run around in circles. Also, drivers were allowed to switch teams between races, so fans often found themselves cheering for a driver that they had booed in the last race. To Pliny, chariot races were silly, not entertaining. To most Romans, however, they were great fun.

SKILL PRACTICE Read the item. Write your response.

1. How is chariot racing like a modern sport? Explain.

2. Was Pliny the Younger a typical Roman? Explain.

3. Name two characteristics that a chariot driver needed to possess.

STRATEGY PRACTICE Describe how you picture the scene of a race at Circus Maximus.

Theme

READ THE PASSAGE — Think about what the author wants you to know about Moe Berg.

The Baseball-Playing Spy

Moe Berg was a scholar and a baseball player. In the 1920s, he turned down an offer to teach at Princeton University so he could play baseball. He was well respected during his 15-year sports career. Teammates often asked him for advice, and sportswriters praised his intelligence. Berg spoke several languages and earned a law degree while playing baseball.

U.S. government officials wanted to put Berg's sharp mind to work during World War II, so they hired him as a spy. In Europe, Berg gathered information about people who were willing to help the United States and its allies in the war against Germany. Berg also questioned top scientist Werner Heisenberg about the German nuclear bomb program. Berg never returned to baseball or had another job after World War II.

Berg was always a mysterious person. There were many theories about him. Some people suspected that he was still employed by the Office of Strategic Services, which later became the Central Intelligence Agency, or CIA. Others suggested that his tales of wartime spy activities were lies. Still others claimed that he had been a spy even during his baseball career. They pointed to the fact that he had always remained just an average player, despite all his years in the Major Leagues. Whenever anyone asked Berg, he just held a finger to his lips, as if to say that it was a secret. One way or another, Moe Berg understood that some things were better left unsaid.

SKILL PRACTICE — Read the item. Write your response.

1. Why did Moe Berg's teammates probably look to him for advice?

2. What is the theme of this text?

3. What message does the author want to convey to the reader?

STRATEGY PRACTICE — Explain how the author's portrayal of Moe Berg changes from the first paragraph to the last paragraph.

READ THE PASSAGE Think about how the author communicates her views about animal care.

Valley Veterinary Clinic

As soon as Rufus got to work on Monday, he noticed the light blinking on the answering machine. He knew there would be several messages. Dr. Tran, Rufus's boss, was the only veterinarian in town, so the clinic was always busy.

Rufus jotted down each message. Ms. Vesey's horse had a cut on its leg and might need antibiotics. Mr. Garland's old hunting dog had developed a limp and needed to have its leg checked. One of Mr. Jamison's ranch cats had caught a mouse and hadn't eaten since then. Rufus smiled. He thought he'd probably seen every pet in the county by now.

Rufus had learned a lot since starting his job as an assistant at the clinic. He learned what questions to ask animal owners, how to enter data into the computer system, and how to process payments. He also knew the names and uses of many animal medications. His favorite part of the job, though, was working with the animals. He knew just where to pat a dog or scratch a cat to comfort it. Even though Rufus hadn't studied veterinary medicine in school, he knew a lot about different kinds of animals. Sometimes he was surprised by how much he knew.

The phone rang and Rufus answered it. The voice on the other end of the line made him smile. "Congratulations, Rosie!" Rufus told the caller. "How old are Midnight's puppies? Sure, Dr. Tran can examine them. Can you bring them by at three o'clock this afternoon?"

SKILL PRACTICE Read the item. Write your response.

1. What is the theme of this text?

2. How does Rufus feel about his job? Cite text evidence to support your response.

3. What does the author show the reader through dialogue in the last paragraph?

STRATEGY PRACTICE Imagine what it would be like to work in this veterinary clinic. Describe how you picture it in your mind.

Character and Setting **WEEK 22**
Theme **DAY 5**

READ THE PASSAGE   Think about what the author wants you to know about the Millau Viaduct.

One Tall Bridge

On a clear December day in 2004, traffic began to travel along the Millau Viaduct (MEE-yo VY-uh-dukt) for the first time. This new suspension bridge was built by Eiffel Iron Company, the same company that built the Eiffel Tower in Paris. It is the tallest bridge in the world, at nearly 900 feet (274 m) above the Tarn River valley in southern France. One of its support pillars is even taller than the Eiffel Tower.

Architect Norman Foster and a team of engineers created the plans for the Millau Viaduct. The goal of the project was to connect the main roadways of Spain and France. Foster's team wanted a strong bridge that did not interfere with the natural beauty of the valley. It was important to them to preserve the landscape.

When viewed from a distance, the roadway of the bridge appears straight. But it is actually slightly curved, which allows travelers to get a full view of the valley around the town of Millau. Engineers used steel instead of concrete to make the curved surface of the road.

Many people would agree that Foster and his team were successful in their goal. On some days, low-lying clouds form between the floor of the valley and the road surface of the bridge. On those days, the view is at least as beautiful as before the bridge was built.

SKILL PRACTICE   Read the item. Write your response.

1. Draw a conclusion about Norman Foster.

2. Why does the author mention the Eiffel Tower twice in the text?

3. Would you like to walk across the Millau Viaduct? Explain.

STRATEGY PRACTICE   What is the central message or theme of the passage? Explain your answer.

Author's Purpose — WEEK 23, DAY 1

READ THE PASSAGE   Think about why the author wrote this passage about an odd inventor.

The Nutty Inventor

In the world of inventions, Yoshiro Nakamatsu deserves the grand prize. "Dr. NakaMats," as he calls himself, has created more than 3,200 inventions during his lifetime. His inventions include the compact disc (CD), the digital watch, a taxicab meter, and spring shoes that allow people to jump high with less effort. Dr. NakaMats proves that great things can happen when people use their imaginations.

How does this brilliant inventor come up with ideas for new inventions? Even he would probably admit that his process is a little strange. Dr. NakaMats starts by diving into a swimming pool. He remains underwater, holding his breath, until an idea comes to him. Then he writes his idea on a special underwater tablet that he invented for just this purpose.

Dr. NakaMats believes that his creativity is at its best between midnight and 4 AM. He sleeps only four hours a day and eats only one meal a day. His habits may seem strange, but the money he earns from his inventions has given him the freedom to work however—and whenever—he pleases. "Genius lies in developing complete and perfect freedom within a human being. Only then can a person come up with the best ideas," he explains.

SKILL PRACTICE   Read the item. Write your response.

1. Why did the author write this text?

2. Why does the author tell the reader how Dr. NakaMats generates new ideas?

3. Predict what Dr. NakaMats will do in the future.

STRATEGY PRACTICE   Write two questions that you would ask Dr. NakaMats if you could.

Author's Purpose

WEEK 23 DAY 2

READ THE PASSAGE Think about the author's purpose as you read about the game of cricket.

Playing Cricket

All you need to play a game of cricket is a bat, a ball, a field, and a group of friends. At first glance, the sport looks a lot like baseball. The basic equipment is the same, although a cricket bat is flat and wide, like a paddle. Also, instead of running around bases, cricket players run back and forth on a strip of ground called a "pitch." The pitcher, who is called a "bowler," stands at one end of the pitch and throws the ball to the batter at the other end.

Cricket can be complicated. The official rules for the game, called "laws," are detailed and exact. There are also many forms of the game, including first-class cricket, in which the game lasts up to five days, and one-day cricket, which lasts just one day. Amateur cricket has many variations. Players often pause during the game to socialize and enjoy refreshments. In this way, the sport combines the excitement of competition with the tradition of a social gathering.

The history of cricket goes back much further than that of baseball. Cricket has been played in England for centuries. English settlers took the sport to Australia, India, and other British colonies. Today, cricket is the most popular sport in India, where televised games attract about 100 million viewers. Cricket may not be well known in the United States, but the game has stood the test of time in many other parts of the world.

SKILL PRACTICE Read the item. Write your response.

1. Why did the author write this text?
   _____
   _____

2. Why did the author explain how cricket is played?
   _____
   _____

3. Would you like to play cricket? Explain your stance.
   _____
   _____

STRATEGY PRACTICE Describe a team sport that you have watched or played, and explain how it compares with cricket.
   _____
   _____

WEEK 23
Prediction — **DAY 3**

READ THE PASSAGE — Use clues from the passage and what you know about today's cars to make predictions about the future of electric cars.

The Drive Toward Electric Cars

Electric cars may seem like a recent invention, but they've been around for years. In the early 1900s, there were more electric cars on the road than there were gas-powered vehicles. At that time, gasoline was expensive compared with other fuels. Once gas prices dropped and new technologies were developed, electric cars went out of fashion in favor of gas-powered cars, which could travel longer distances without stopping.

During the 20th century, gas-powered cars got bigger, heavier, and faster. They required more fuel, which led to more air pollution. For years, carmakers didn't worry about pollution. They weren't concerned about how much gas cars used. But as consumers became aware of Earth's limited supply of oil, they pressured manufacturers to make more efficient and less polluting cars.

One solution was a "hybrid" car, one that ran partly on gas and partly on electricity supplied by a battery. Hybrid cars became popular in the mid-2000s as gas prices rose dramatically and car manufacturers made the fuel-efficient cars more affordable.

An all-electric car uses no gasoline. The challenge, though, is that car batteries need to be recharged. That makes electric cars impractical for long distances. The government and car manufacturers are working together to develop safe, inexpensive, and more practical electric cars. Once these cars become available to consumers, gas stations may someday be a thing of the past.

SKILL PRACTICE — Read the item. Write your response.

1. After reading the first two paragraphs, what prediction did you make?

2. Why are hybrid cars more practical than all-electric cars?

3. What might make gas stations become a thing of the past?

STRATEGY PRACTICE — Write two questions that you would ask an engineer who works for a carmaker.

WEEK 23 — Prediction — DAY 4

READ THE PASSAGE Predict what will happen on Misha's first airplane trip.

First Flight

Misha stepped inside the airplane and wrinkled her nose. The plane smelled like the inside of the bus that she had taken to see her grandmother last year. The air was also stuffy, and people sitting in their seats looked grumpy and tired.

Misha checked her ticket and found her seat, but a tall man was already sitting there. Misha sighed loudly. "Excuse me," Misha said. "You're in my seat. I have 19C."

"This is 18C," the man replied. Misha felt her face burn with embarrassment as she scooted into the correct row and scrunched down in the narrow seat. Misha's mother patted Misha on the shoulder and took the seat beside her.

"I already hate planes," Misha pouted as she buckled her seat belt. "I thought this was supposed to be nice, but it's worse than a bus. At least you can open the windows on the bus."

"This trip would take too long by bus," Misha's mother said. "Anyway, they'll turn on the air conditioning soon. Then it won't be so stuffy. Just wait until we take off. As the plane climbs, it'll seem like the world is shrinking before your eyes."

"No thanks," Misha said, pulling her portable DVD player from her bag. "I just want to watch a movie." As soon as Misha turned on her DVD player, the flight attendant frowned and began walking toward Misha's row.

SKILL PRACTICE Read the item. Write your response.

1. Why was Misha embarrassed?

2. Has Misha's mother been on a plane before? How did you draw that conclusion?

3. What will the flight attendant probably do next?

STRATEGY PRACTICE Think of a time when you felt annoyed or uncomfortable. Based on that experience, what advice would you give Misha?

Author's Purpose — Prediction
WEEK 23 DAY 5

READ THE PASSAGE Think about why the author includes certain information in the story. Use clues to make predictions.

Artist's Block

Emily had been staring at the bowl of fruit for the past ten minutes. Her art supplies lay in front of her, untouched. She had a tray of watercolors, a jar of paintbrushes, a shallow pan of water, and a tablet of rough-surfaced paper. Yuki leaned over and nudged her friend. "Emily, what's wrong?" she asked. "You've just been sitting there for 10 minutes."

"I can't figure out how to start," Emily said. She picked up a paintbrush and put it down again. "Artists make this painting stuff look so easy. How do they do it?"

"Start with anything!" Yuki said. "Try painting the bowl first. Then add the fruit."

Emily shook her head. "I'm afraid I'll mess up the shape of the bowl. Then I won't have room for the fruit. I don't know how to get the colors, sizes, and shadows right. You've been painting this whole time. I'll bet yours looks great."

"Oh yeah?" said Yuki. She turned her own tablet around so Emily could see what she'd been painting. Yuki and Emily were using the same subject for a still-life painting. It was a bowl of apples, bananas, and pears. But in Yuki's painting, the bowl was lime green, not brown. And it was filled with odd shapes in purples and pinks. "I call it 'Fruit Bowl on Mars,'" Yuki said proudly. "It's a work in progress. Do you like it?"

Emily laughed and picked up her paintbrush. "I do," she said. "I really do."

SKILL PRACTICE Read the item. Write your response.

1. What is the author's purpose in the first paragraph?

2. Why did the author include the description of Yuki's painting?

3. What will probably happen next?

STRATEGY PRACTICE Write a question that you would ask Yuki or Emily about painting.

Nonfiction Text Features

WEEK 24 DAY 1

READ THE INFORMATION Study the table of contents and read the excerpt from a science text.

Contents

Introduction	i
Chapter 1 The Sun	1
Chapter 2 Mercury	17
Chapter 3 Venus	33
Chapter 4 Earth	45
Chapter 5 The Moon	52
Chapter 6 Mars	66
Chapter 7 Jupiter	72
Chapter 8 Saturn	80
Chapter 9 Uranus	85
Chapter 10 Neptune	92
Chapter 11 Asteroids	98
Chapter 12 Beyond Asteroids	99
Index	104

An Icy Mass

At the far reaches of the solar system, beyond Neptune's orbit, a dark mass of ice orbits the sun. The mass is Pluto, once known as the smallest planet of Earth's solar system. In 2006, astronomers classified Pluto as a dwarf planet.

Although its great distance from Earth makes it difficult for astronomers to study, we do know some things about Pluto. For example, this dwarf planet is only about two-thirds the size of Earth's moon. We also know that Pluto rotates very slowly on its axis. During one day on Pluto, six days pass on Earth.

We know, too, that it takes 248 years for Pluto to orbit the sun. The path it takes brings it inside Neptune's orbit of the sun for several years at a time. In other words, during this period, Pluto is closer to the sun—and to Earth—than Neptune is.

SKILL PRACTICE Read the item. Write your response.

1. What would be a good title for this book and why?

2. On which page could you start reading about NASA's missions to the moon? Explain your choice.

3. To which chapter would you turn to read about solar flares? Explain your choice.

STRATEGY PRACTICE Explain why scientists don't know much about Pluto. Then list two facts that we know.

Nonfiction Text Features — WEEK 24, DAY 2

READ THE INTERVIEW Notice how Carlos Martin responds to the interviewer's questions.

Carlos Martin, Firefighter

Kids Careers caught up with Carlos Martin at his fire station in Dusterville, Iowa.

Kids Careers: Walk us through a day in the life of a small-town firefighter.

Carlos: Much of the day is fairly uneventful. In the morning, I make coffee. Then I check the truck and equipment, make sure the logbook is up to date, and straighten up the kitchen. Most of our daily duties involve making sure the station is tidy. We spend a lot of time here, including sleeping and eating.

Kids Careers: What's the most common type of call you get on an average day?

Carlos: Most calls aren't emergencies. For example, Mrs. Epstein calls us whenever she burns dinner accidentally. She has a sensitive smoke detector, and she can't reach it to turn off the alarm.

Kids Careers: What's the best part of working as a firefighter?

Carlos: Being on a team with skilled people. They've become my good friends. We're like a family.

Kids Careers: What's the worst fire that you've seen?

Carlos: During my first week on the job, we were called out to a tanker truck that had caught fire on the highway. Only the front part was on fire, but we had to work fast because the tanker was full of gasoline. It was a tough situation, but my team and I took care of it safely. That's when I knew I had made the right decision to become a firefighter.

Kids Careers: What advice do you have for kids who want to be firefighters?

Carlos: Get good grades, stay physically fit, and be a good community member. Firefighters are there to help people, and I think it's the best job in the world.

SKILL PRACTICE Read the item. Write your response.

1. Where does this interview take place?

_____

_____

2. What made the tanker truck fire the worst that Carlos has seen?

_____

_____

3. What do you think *Kids Careers* is? Explain.

_____

STRATEGY PRACTICE Write a related question that the interviewer might ask after hearing about the tanker truck fire. Have a partner answer it as if he or she is Carlos Martin.

_____

_____

READ THE PASSAGE Notice how the information in the diagram and the text support each other.

How a Tsunami Forms

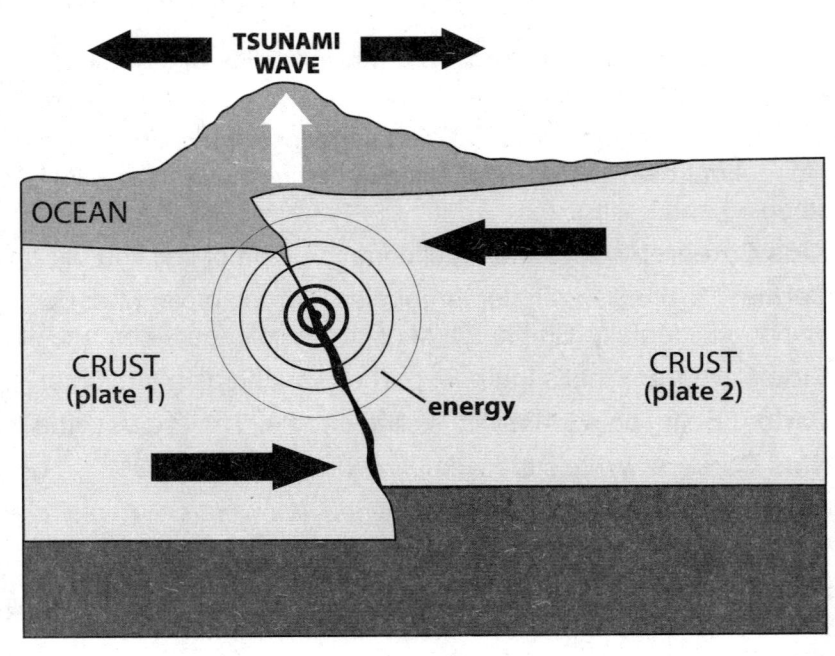

A *tsunami* (soo-NAH-mee) is a massive ocean wave usually caused by an earthquake beneath the ocean. Most earthquakes occur where two plates, or blocks of Earth's crust, come together. When the plates push against each other, one plate can snap up suddenly, releasing energy upward. The energy is then transferred into the ocean, causing a tsunami wave to rise and spread out in two directions. In deeper water, the wave moves faster and farther than in shallow water. A tsunami can travel thousands of miles before it reaches the shore.

SKILL PRACTICE Read the item. Write your response.

1. What do the circles in the middle of the diagram indicate?
   _____
   _____

2. What happens to the wave of water caused by an undersea earthquake?
   _____
   _____

3. Where would you be likely to see this text and diagram?
   _____

STRATEGY PRACTICE Write a short caption for the diagram to summarize how an earthquake can cause a tsunami.

_____
_____

Visual Information — WEEK 24, DAY 4

READ THE GRAPH Think about the information in the graph.

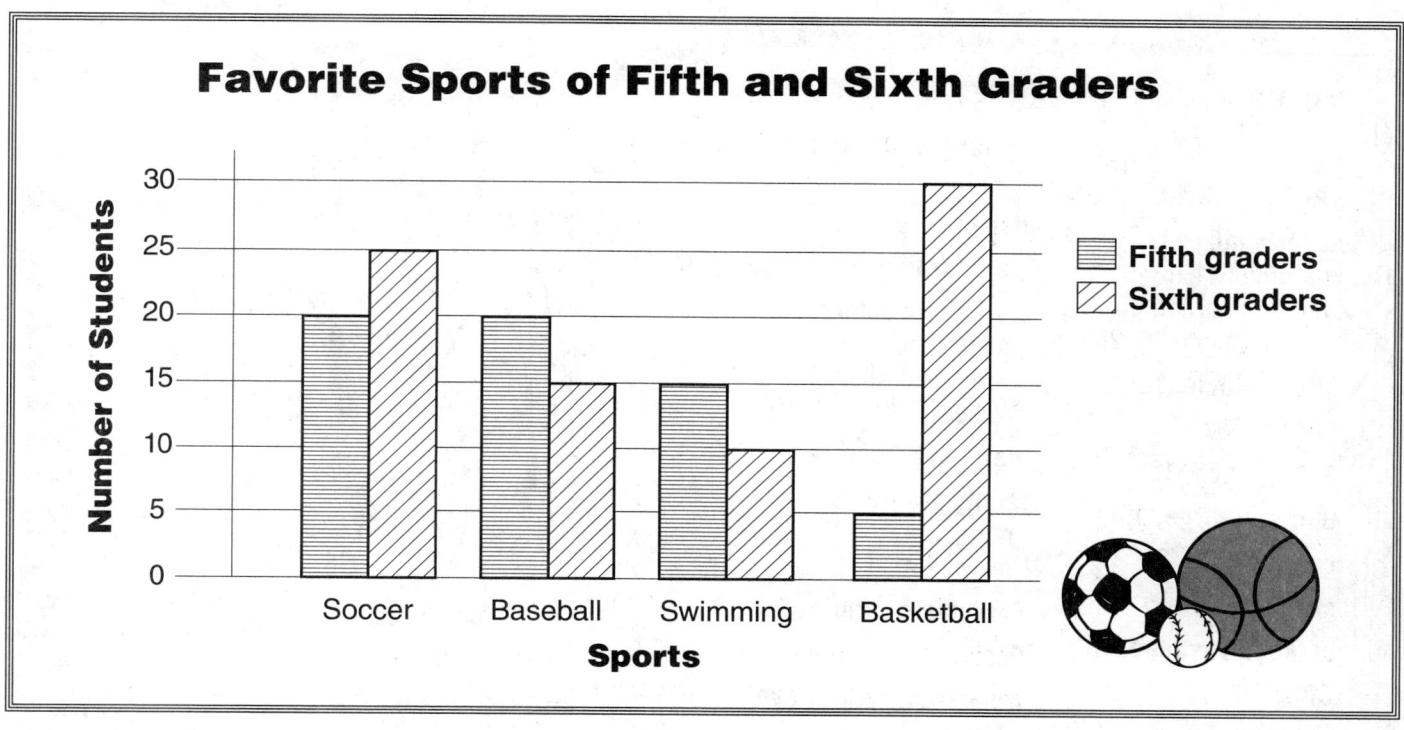

SKILL PRACTICE Read the item. Write your response.

1. Which sports are more popular with fifth graders than sixth graders?

2. The same number of fifth graders voted for which two sports as their favorites?

3. How many fifth graders were polled? How many sixth graders? How do you know?

STRATEGY PRACTICE How would you change this graph to compare favorite sports for grades 5, 6, and 7?

Nonfiction Text Features — **WEEK 24**
Visual Information — **DAY 5**

READ THE INDEX — Study the index and paragraph from a book about the history of broadcasting.

INDEX
(A–C)
ABC, 12, 27
advertising
 on radio, 11, 13
 on the Internet, 60
 on television, 26, 28
Allen, Gracie, 16
BBC, 18, 37
Benny, Jack, 18
Burns, George, 16
cable TV, 38–39
cartoons, 26–27
cathode-ray tube, 25
CBS, 11, 27
color TV, 30
Communications Act
 of 1934, 18

(D–F)
digital broadcasting
 24, 40, 42
dish (see *satellite*)
drama, radio, 14–15, 19
early radio actors
 Benny, Jack, 18
 Burns and Allen, 16
 Welles, Orson, 14–15
electron tubes, 25
family programs
 radio, 8
 television, 26–27
Farnsworth, Philo, 25
Fessenden, Reginald, 5
frequency, radio wave
 AM, 6, 17
 FM, 18, 61

During the 1930s, actors competed for the best parts in radio plays. Orson Welles's performance in the radio drama *War of the Worlds*, about Martians invading Earth, attracted six million listeners.

SKILL PRACTICE — Read the item. Write your response.

1. Who does the illustration show, and what is he doing?

_____

_____

2. Describe what you would read about on page 6.

_____

_____

3. Consider the focus of the book that has this index. Name a show you might read about on pages 26 and 27.

_____

STRATEGY PRACTICE — Describe the type of person who might find this book helpful.

_____

WEEK 25 — Main Idea and Details — DAY 1

READ THE PASSAGE Look for details that help you understand more about Victor and Julie.

Working in the Sky

Victor tucked a rag into his pocket and picked up the bucket. Then he and his new coworker, Julie, lowered the platform down another floor. The window washers were 200 feet (61 m) in the air, and Julie peered over the safety rails at the people and cars on the street below. A sudden gust of wind caused the platform to sway, and Julie quickly jumped back.

"Still nervous?" Victor asked.

"A little," Julie said.

Victor dunked his squeegee into the bucket of soapy water on the platform and wet the window with its sponge. "It takes a week or two to get used to being up here," he said. "It also helps not to look down all the time." Julie watched him drag the squeegee's rubber blade across the window.

Julie ran her fingers along the strap of her safety harness. "Have you ever fallen off?"

"Never," Victor said. "And I don't know anyone who has. These harnesses never really get used." He tapped the buckle of his own harness. After a few more passes with the squeegee blade, the window was clean. Victor lowered the platform to the next floor.

"Okay," Victor said as he handed the cleaning tools to Julie. "Let's see what you can do."

Julie smiled as she took the squeegee, thankful for something to focus her attention on.

SKILL PRACTICE Read the item. Write your response.

1. What is the squeegee used for?

2. Cite text evidence that shows how Julie feels about her job. Use quotations marks.

3. What is the main idea of this text?

STRATEGY PRACTICE Write two important details about Victor or Julie. Explain why these details are important.

Main Idea and Details — WEEK 25, DAY 2

READ THE PASSAGE Look for details that explain why Buster Keaton is considered to be original.

An Original Hollywood Star

In the early days of Hollywood, films were just moving pictures without sound. Actors, therefore, could not rely on their voices to express ideas and emotions. Instead, they used their faces and body language. The best actors were usually the ones with the most expressive faces.

Buster Keaton, though, was different from most silent film actors. Keaton almost always wore a blank expression on his face. And the characters he played often found themselves in funny situations. His expressionless face, combined with the physical humor and funny situations in the films, was a hit with audiences.

Keaton first appeared on stage with his parents when he was nine months old. His movie career began at the age of 22. He acted in 35 short films over a five-year period. He began making full-length feature films in 1923 and was known for being willing to try anything new in his films. Some of his films featured expensive and, for their time, wonderful special effects. Keaton did all of his own stunts, and he often wrote and directed the films in which he starred.

Buster Keaton's film career continued until his death in 1966. Many of his most successful movies have been preserved, so new generations can still enjoy his original acting and storytelling.

SKILL PRACTICE Read the item. Write your response.

1. Write the main idea of this text in your own words.
   _____
   _____

2. What detail from the text supports the title?
   _____
   _____

3. What is the author's purpose for writing the first paragraph?
   _____
   _____

STRATEGY PRACTICE Write words or phrases from the passage that were easy to visualize.
   _____
   _____

Sequence

WEEK 25 DAY 3

READ THE PASSAGE Think about the sequence of events in building the Mount Rushmore memorial.

Carving History

In 1927, artists and engineers began using dynamite to blast the mountain peak of Mount Rushmore in the Black Hills of South Dakota. People had been using dynamite to clear away rock from mountains for years, but this blast was special. The engineers were not mining, digging a tunnel, or building a road. They were using Mount Rushmore as a monument to honor four great American leaders. The project was the Mount Rushmore National Memorial.

South Dakota state historian Doane Robinson and sculptor Gutzon Borglum planned the memorial project, raised money for it, and chose its location. They decided to carve four portraits of past presidents—George Washington, Thomas Jefferson, Abraham Lincoln, and Theodore Roosevelt. Each portrait was finished in secret and then revealed during a special celebration.

The carving of George Washington was finished first and revealed on July 4, 1934. The carving of Jefferson was shown in 1936. The carving of Lincoln was revealed in September 1937, and the carving of Roosevelt was shown to the public in 1939. That same year, modern plumbing and night lighting were installed nearby for visitors. By the time the monument was completed, the cost was more than one million dollars, which would be equal to more than ten million dollars in today's money.

Funding for the memorial ran out in 1941, just as the final details were being finished. According to the sculptor, the carvings will remain on Mount Rushmore, "until the wind and the rain alone shall wear them away." Today, Mount Rushmore receives more than two million visitors each year who want to see an inspiring work of art.

SKILL PRACTICE Read the item. Write your response.

1. Which president's sculpture was the first to be revealed?

_____

2. Why do you think that the sculptures were completed in the order that they were?

_____

_____

3. Can the monument be viewed at night? Explain.

_____

_____

STRATEGY PRACTICE Underline the details in the passage that explain why the memorial at Mount Rushmore took so many years to complete.

Sequence — WEEK 25, DAY 4

READ THE PASSAGE Pay attention to the information that tells you how the Maya counted and named days.

The Mayan Calendar

The Mayan people of Central and South America created an accurate calendar thousands of years ago. Their calendar, like ours, named the days and the months. But the Maya had different systems for counting days.

One system the Maya used was called the *Tzolkin*. The system had a religious calendar with a 260-day cycle. The Maya used a combination of numbers and names—like our Monday, Tuesday, Wednesday, and so on—to refer to the days. The system had 20 day names—Imix, Ik, Akbal, Kan, Chicchan, and so on until day 20, called Ahau—which followed the same sequence in a cycle. Days were also numbered 1 to 13. The fourteenth day in a sequence began with 1 again. So, if today were *1 Imix,* then tomorrow would be *2 Ik,* and the next day would be *3 Akbal.* Nineteen days from *1 Imix,* would be *7 Ahau,* and the day after that would be *8 Imix.*

The system that kept track of months was called the *Haab.* A year in the Haab system had 18 months, each with 20 days, making a total of 360 days. The names of the first five months, in sequence, were Pop, Uo, Zip, Zotz, and Tzec. The Maya referred to days of the month using numbers 0 to 19, in sequence, and then the month name. So, instead of January 1, the Maya had *0 Pop.* The day after *0 Pop* was *1 Pop,* and the last day of that month was *19 Pop.*

The Maya knew that a year lasted 365 days, so they added five days at the end of the Haab cycle. These days were called *Uayeb* and were considered to be bad luck. The way that the Maya recorded time may seem strange, but their calendar was nearly as accurate as ours is today.

SKILL PRACTICE Read the item. Write your response.

1. In the Haab system, what day comes after 19 Pop? How can you tell?

2. How could the Maya fit 18 months into a year?

3. How do we know that the Maya realized there are 365 days in a year?

STRATEGY PRACTICE Draw a calendar that shows the days in the month of Uo.

Main Idea and Details — **WEEK 25**
Sequence — **DAY 5**

READ THE PASSAGE Think about the main idea, details, and sequence of the passage.

Shelter Days

Olivia enjoys working at the animal shelter near the park. She has only one dog at home, but at the shelter she has more than 50! The shelter dogs are mostly well-behaved, and they love all the attention Olivia gives them.

When Olivia arrives at the shelter in the morning, she goes to each cage and greets each dog. Breakfast—kibble and water—comes next. After that, each dog gets some exercise. On most mornings, the bigger dogs play together in the shelter yard. Olivia chases the dogs around the yard or plays fetch with them. After playtime, Olivia brushes each dog's coat and puts the dog back into its kennel.

Olivia sweeps the shelter floors while the dogs rest. There is always dirt and hair on the floor because of all the dogs running around. After cleaning, Olivia takes any dog that needs its shots to the shelter vet. At the end of the day, Olivia fills out paperwork before heading home.

Olivia does not get paid for her time at the shelter, but the time she spends with so many good dogs is worth more than money. When someone adopts a dog from the shelter, Olivia feels a little sad to see the dog go. But she is also happy to see one of her furry friends find a forever home.

SKILL PRACTICE Read the item. Write your response.

1. What does Olivia do right before she puts the dogs into their cages?

   _____
   _____

2. When does Olivia complete paperwork?

   _____
   _____

3. Cite text evidence that tells you how Olivia feels about volunteering. Use quotation marks.

   _____
   _____

STRATEGY PRACTICE Make a timeline that shows what a typical day at the shelter is like for Olivia.

Cause and Effect — WEEK 26, DAY 1

READ THE PASSAGE Think about how Cai Lun's discovery affected China and the rest of the world.

The Paper Man

Before paper was invented, people wrote or drew on materials such as bamboo, silk, animal hide, and wooden blocks. Some cultures even used chisels to carve marks on pieces of stone. Writing materials were expensive and hard to use, and few people learned to read. Therefore, few people wrote. This all changed, thanks to a man named Cai Lun.

Cai Lun began working as a palace servant in Imperial China in the year AD 75. His service to the emperor was rewarded with several promotions. Cai Lun's most important promotion came in the year 89, when he was put in charge of making paper.

Paper had already existed in China, but the process for making it was difficult and the paper was low quality. Cai Lun began experimenting with many different materials and different ways of reducing those materials to paper.

In the year 105, Cai Lun showed the emperor a way of making paper from tree bark, bamboo, cloth rags, and fishing nets. Cai Lun's paper was stronger and cheaper than any paper that had been made before. The emperor was pleased and gave Cai Lun great wealth.

Because of Cai Lun's papermaking method, Chinese culture grew more rapidly over the next several centuries. That's because ideas were much easier to share, and more people learned to read. The use of paper spread beyond China, helping other cultures record and spread their ideas. Today, Cai Lun is considered a national hero in China. But the entire world should be grateful for the clever Chinese papermaker.

SKILL PRACTICE Read the item. Write your response.

1. What was the result of Cai Lun's experiments?

_____

_____

2. Do you think that Cai Lun realized the effect his experiments would have on the world?

_____

_____

3. How did Cai Lun's discovery allow Chinese culture to grow more rapidly? Be specific.

_____

_____

STRATEGY PRACTICE Underline sentences in the passage that tell why Cai Lun's discovery was valuable.

WEEK 26 DAY 2

Cause and Effect

READ THE PASSAGE   Identify Gretchen's actions in the story and the effects of those actions.

Horses

Before taking a summer job at Circle J Ranch, Gretchen hadn't spent much time around horses. During her first couple of weeks on the job, she learned how to feed and care for the animals. Gretchen learned that the horses received a special blend of feed to keep their hooves strong and their manes and coats shiny. Gretchen brushed the horses every day and sometimes gave them carrots and apples. These treats calmed the horses during grooming, so they eventually began to trust Gretchen.

After learning how to care for the horses, Gretchen learned how to ride. The horses at Circle J were very well trained for riding. They walked when the rider touched her heels to their sides, and they stopped right away when the rider pulled gently on the reins. Soon, Gretchen was nearly as comfortable on a horse as she was on her own two feet.

Before the summer was over, Gretchen had become fond of all the horses at the ranch. The owners told her that she had done a great job and they hoped to see her again next summer. They also told her that she was welcome to visit Circle J anytime.

Gretchen began thinking of ways she could ask her parents for her own horse, but she doubted they would give her one. She decided that she would bring them to the ranch one day. When they saw how well she got along with the horses, she felt sure they would at least consider her request.

SKILL PRACTICE   Read the item. Write your response.

1. What signal does Gretchen use to tell the horse to start walking? To stop walking?

_____

_____

2. Why did the Circle J Ranch owners invite Gretchen to work there again the next summer?

_____

_____

3. What will Gretchen do next?

_____

STRATEGY PRACTICE   Write a question you thought of while reading the passage. If you found the answer, write it, too.

_____

_____

Week 26 — Fact and Opinion — Day 3

READ THE PASSAGE Identify the facts and the statements of opinion about candles.

Little Firelights

Candles may be the most important indoor invention ever. They are portable little fires that brighten the night. Before electricity, candles were the most common way to light up a dark room. Countless letters, books, and poems have been written—and read—by candlelight.

The origin of the candle is something of a mystery. It is commonly believed that the earliest candles were made from cooked animal fat called *tallow.* Ancient Egyptians used primitive candles called *rushlights,* which were made from the stems of plant reeds dipped in tallow. Ancient Romans invented the wick, which burned better and longer, to replace the reed stem.

Odor was a problem with early candles. Tallow gives off an unpleasant smell when it is burned. In the Middle Ages, people discovered that beeswax could be used instead of tallow. Beeswax gives off almost no odor, but it was so rare that only the wealthy could afford it. Women in colonial America discovered that boiled bayberries produced a sweet-smelling wax that could be used to make candles, but the wax was difficult to get from the berries. Bayberry-wax candles are rare. However, bayberry-scented candles are still popular today.

Most modern candles are made from *paraffin,* an artificial mixture of oils that is plentiful and inexpensive. Some people prefer candles made from natural soy or beeswax, however.

SKILL PRACTICE Read the item. Write your response.

1. Are there any opinions in the second paragraph? How can you tell?

_____

_____

2. Which sentence in the first paragraph can be proven true? Use quotation marks.

_____

_____

3. How do today's candles differ from those used in the Middle Ages?

_____

STRATEGY PRACTICE Think about what someone might want to know before buying a candle. Write one fact and one opinion about each type of wax mentioned in the passage.

_____

_____

_____

Fact and Opinion

WEEK 26 DAY 4

READ THE PASSAGE Decide which statements about bacteria are fact and which show an opinion.

Bacteria

The smallest living creatures on Earth are bacteria. In fact, you can't see them without a microscope. Bacteria may be small, but there are a *lot* of them! An ounce (28 g) of soil, for example, may contain more than a billion of these organisms!

Bacteria have been on this planet for a long time. In fact, the oldest known fossils are full of bacteria. These organisms can also survive where others cannot. Bacteria have been found in cold places such as in deep Arctic ice and in hot places such as the insides of geysers.

We tend to think of bacteria only as "germs" that make us sick, but bacteria do many things that help life on Earth survive and thrive. They help break down dead plants and animals into soil nutrients. Without these nutrients, soil could not be used to grow food for humans and animals. Without bacteria, ecosystems would be less healthy because dead plants and animals would not break down properly.

Bacteria are also responsible for the flavor and texture of some foods. They affect the taste of some types of bread, for example. And without bacteria we would not have cheese or yogurt.

The human body needs some bacteria to function properly. Microscopic bacteria in our stomachs and intestines help us digest food. In addition, bacteria help remove dead skin cells so our pores can breathe. And some kinds of bacteria even fight off other kinds of bacteria that can make us ill. Scientists, in fact, use bacteria to make medicines that help us recover from illnesses. Bacteria just might be the most beneficial organisms on Earth!

SKILL PRACTICE Read the item. Write your response.

1. Name three ways in which bacteria help humans.

_____

_____

2. How do bacteria benefit ecosystems?

_____

_____

3. Are there any opinions in the last paragraph? How can you tell?

_____

STRATEGY PRACTICE Write a question about bacteria that can be answered using information from the passage.

_____

Cause and Effect — WEEK 26
Fact and Opinion — DAY 5

READ THE PASSAGE Think about causes and effects, as well as facts and opinions, as you read.

A Quick Snack

Grilled cheese sandwiches are a great option for lunch when there isn't a lot of time to cook. They're quick, easy, and tasty. All you need to make one is some cheese, two slices of bread, some butter or oil, a pan, and a stove.

First, put a little butter or oil in the pan. This will help the bread toast evenly and prevent it from sticking to the pan. You can also spread butter directly on the bread. This can be tricky, though, because the butter can make your fingers slippery as you put the sandwich together.

The next step is to put cheese between the slices of bread. Grilled cheese sandwiches can be made with any kind of cheese you want, as long as it melts easily. Cheddar cheese is the most popular choice, but Monterey Jack is good, too. Some people like to add vegetables or a few slices of tomato to their sandwiches along with the cheese.

Now it's time to get cooking. Heat the butter or oil in the pan. Cook the sandwich over medium heat until the bread is toasted and the cheese begins to melt. Using high heat will burn the bread. Using a spatula, flip the sandwich to toast the other slice of bread. By the time the heat has made both slices of bread crispy, the cheese inside should be melted. The melted cheese will also seal in any vegetables you added. Slide or lift your sandwich onto a plate and enjoy it!

SKILL PRACTICE Read the item. Write your response.

1. Amal is making a grilled cheese sandwich. The bread burns before the cheese melts. What did she do wrong?

   _____
   _____

2. How many sentences in the first paragraph are facts? Explain.

   _____
   _____

3. Can you use pepper jack cheese to make a grilled cheese sandwich? How can you tell?

   _____
   _____

STRATEGY PRACTICE Write the steps, in order, for making a grilled cheese sandwich.

   _____
   _____

Compare and Contrast — WEEK 27, DAY 1

READ THE PASSAGE   Think about how Terry, Maria, and Patty are similar and different.

Patty's Home Sweet Home

"Patty's Home Sweet Home" is a large furniture store at the south end of town. The building is divided into sections for different parts of a home, including a bedroom and a kitchen. Organizing the store this way helps employees keep track of the goods they sell. It also helps customers quickly find what they need.

Terry works in the bedroom section. When people come to look for a new bed, he invites them to sit on the mattresses to compare them. He suggests that customers open and close dresser drawers to see how quietly they glide. Terry wants customers to test the furniture so they know what they are buying.

The kitchen section is where Maria works. She knows all about different types of stoves, sinks, and dishwashers. Customers in the kitchen section can ask Maria anything about these appliances. She wants to make sure that her customers get all the information they need about the products they're planning to buy.

Patty owns the store. She moves from section to section to make sure everything is running smoothly. She spends most of her time chatting with customers and making sure their shopping experience is going well. Sometimes she helps her salespeople, but they don't usually need help. The salespeople at Patty's store do their jobs well, and customers seem satisfied.

SKILL PRACTICE   Read the item. Write your response.

1. Write two goals shared by Terry, Maria, and Patty.

2. Could Terry and Maria switch jobs for a day? Explain.

3. How is Patty different from both Terry and Maria?

STRATEGY PRACTICE   Would you act more like Terry, Maria, or Patty? Why?

Compare and Contrast — WEEK 27, DAY 2

READ THE PASSAGE Think about the job of each archaeologist.

The Many Sides of Archaeology

Do you enjoy learning about life in the past? If so, you might consider a career in archaeology when you grow up. Archaeologists are scientists who study human life and cultures of the past.

Some archaeologists work outside on field crews, digging and searching where people lived long ago. Field crews uncover all kinds of things from the past, including homes, roads, tools, art objects, and even garbage pits.

Archaeologists often specialize in certain areas of study. One kind of archaeologist, for example, studies the remains of animals from sites where humans lived long ago. They want to know more about the animals that people hunted, raised for food, or kept as companions.

Some archaeologists study the remains of shipwrecks. They look for clues that explain why the wrecks occurred. The treasures they find at the bottom of the ocean can reveal where people traveled, how they got there, and whom they traded goods with.

Not all archaeologists work outdoors. Some work at museums, universities, or parks. They study the records that other archaeologists create and help preserve the artifacts that field crews dig up. These specialists not only discover secrets about life long ago, but they also help the public to understand those discoveries.

SKILL PRACTICE Read the item. Write your response.

1. What is the common goal of all archaeologists?

   _____

   _____

2. How are archaeologists who study shipwrecks similar to those on field crews?

   _____

   _____

3. In what ways does an archaeologist who works at a museum different from a field archaeologist?

   _____

   _____

STRATEGY PRACTICE Make a chart that shows the different types of archaeologists and tells something important about each of their jobs.

Make Inferences — WEEK 27 DAY 3

READ THE PASSAGE Use text clues and background knowledge to make inferences about marathons.

Run, Run, Run

A marathon is one of the most challenging events in the sport of running. Competitors run a distance of 26.2 miles (42 km), and the first person to cross the finish line wins. People who run marathons train hard to build the endurance they need for such a long race. So far, no one has finished a marathon in less than two hours.

The idea for the race comes from an ancient Greek legend set at the historic Battle of Marathon. The Greek army was badly outnumbered by the Persian army. Nevertheless, the Greeks won. A messenger was so excited about the victory that he ran without stopping all the way from Marathon to the city of Athens to deliver the news. The distance he covered was about 26 miles (42 km). In the legend, the messenger died suddenly after arriving.

Many people believe that just finishing a marathon is a triumph. The human body uses a great deal of energy to run long distances. Nearly all marathon runners experience something called "hitting the wall" near the end of the race. This is a runner's term for getting extremely tired suddenly. The body runs out of sugars to use for energy and starts to burn fats. The runner feels very tired until his or her body begins to turn fats into fuel.

Marathons are about more than competition. The winner of the 1952 Olympic marathon said this about the sport: "If you want to win something, run 100 meters. If you want to experience something, run a marathon."

SKILL PRACTICE Read the item. Write your response.

1. How was the length of a marathon selected?

___

2. Why do many marathon runners "hit the wall"?

___

3. Why did the ancient Greek messenger probably die suddenly?

___

STRATEGY PRACTICE Give at least two reasons that a person might run a marathon.

___

Make Inferences — WEEK 27 DAY 4

READ THE PASSAGE Use clues from the passage to make inferences about Spanish history.

Spain's First Queen

You probably know that the United States began as a few small colonies. But did you know that many other countries began in the same way? Spain, located in Europe, was one such country. Its history was shaped by a young woman named Isabella.

Isabella was born on April 22, 1451. Her father was the king of Castile, a kingdom that was part of Spain. Sadly, the king died when Isabella was only three years old. Her brother, Henry IV, then ruled the kingdom, but he named Isabella as heir to the throne—at first, anyway.

King Henry searched for a husband for the young Isabella so she could someday become queen. But Isabella did not want to marry any of the men that Henry chose for her. Instead, she wanted to marry Ferdinand, the king of Aragon, which was another part of Spain. Isabella fled the castle and hid in a small village until she and Ferdinand could be married.

Henry disapproved of the marriage, so he decided to name his own daughter, Joan, as heir to the throne. When Henry died in 1474, both Joan and Isabella claimed the throne, which started a civil war. When the war ended in 1479, Isabella became queen of Castile, and Ferdinand became king.

Another war began later in Isabella's reign, this time to bring the kingdom of Granada into the already united kingdoms of Aragon and Castile. It was during this war that Christopher Columbus asked Isabella to fund his journey to America. Spain was finally united in February 1492, just a few months before Columbus set sail.

SKILL PRACTICE Read the item. Write your response.

1. Was it important to Isabella that she please Henry IV? Explain.

   _____

   _____

2. How did Queen Isabella affect the history of the United States?

   _____

   _____

3. What can you infer about Isabella from the text's title?

   _____

   _____

STRATEGY PRACTICE Make a timeline of important events in Isabella's life.

Compare and Contrast | **WEEK 27**
Make Inferences | **DAY 5**

READ THE PASSAGE — Compare different kinds of beetles and make inferences about them.

Bunches of Beetles

Almost everyone has seen a beetle at some time in their lives. These insects lurk in garden beds or feed on blooming trees in the summertime. They often enter houses. Almost anywhere humans go, beetles can follow.

There are more than 300,000 different kinds of beetles on Earth, and they all have some similarities. For example, all beetles have six legs and two antennae. And their bodies are divided into three segments. Beetles share these characteristics with all other insects, as well.

There are also differences among species of beetles. Some beetles, such as ladybugs and fiddler beetles, can fly. Other species, such as the ironclad beetle, can only walk. Beetles also vary greatly in size. Some are about the size of a grain of sand. In contrast, titan beetles from South American rainforests can grow to more than 6 inches (15 cm) in length.

Beetles have different ways of defending themselves. Bombardier (bom-bur-DEER) beetles have special glands in their bodies that spray a hot chemical to warn predators. Acrobat beetles scare predators by doing headstands. Still other types of beetles, such as leaf beetles, hide by blending in with their surroundings. This form of defense is known as *camouflage.*

Most beetles are harmless—or even helpful—to humans. Ladybugs, for example, feed on pests that damage crops. Given the number of beetles in the world, it is a good thing that humans get along with most of them!

SKILL PRACTICE — Read the item. Write your response.

1. How are ladybugs and fiddler beetles alike?

   _____

   _____

2. What do beetles have in common with all other insects?

   _____

3. Based on the text, which beetle can you infer is the largest in length on Earth? Explain.

   _____

   _____

STRATEGY PRACTICE — Explain how remembering beetles you have seen helped you understand the passage.

_____

_____

Character and Setting — WEEK 28, DAY 1

READ THE PASSAGE Think about how Ashoka changed and what effect the change had on others.

Good Emperor Ashoka

Many cultures have stories about gentle, wise, and kind rulers. Most of these stories are legends. They were not meant to be historical records. Instead, these stories were meant to help people endure cruel or greedy rulers and give them hope for the future.

In southern Asia, however, a beloved ruler really did exist. His name was Ashoka the Great, and he brought peace to a region that is now India, Bangladesh, and Pakistan. Ashoka was so well liked that some of the symbols he used during his reign—lions that stood for power, courage, and confidence—remain national symbols of India.

Ashoka the Great had not always been kind. For several years he had ruled no differently from the long line of cruel kings and warlords that came before him. However, after Ashoka witnessed the terrible results of the Kalinga War, which destroyed the land and killed many thousands of people, he changed. Ashoka realized that conquest also brings great suffering, so he sent a message of respect and nonviolence to the farthest corners of his kingdom.

The message impressed people, not just for its ideas but for the message itself. The language Ashoka used was plain, sincere, and personal. Ashoka wanted everyone to understand the values he learned through the hard lessons of war.

SKILL PRACTICE Read the item. Write your response.

1. How did Ashoka change after experiencing the Kalinga War?

2. Where did the events in this text occur?

3. Which modern country has adopted symbols from Ashoka the Great?

STRATEGY PRACTICE Tell how the first sentence of paragraphs 2, 3, and 4 helped you better understand the ideas in the passage.

WEEK 28
Character and Setting DAY 2

READ THE PASSAGE Think about how Jin and Laurie behave in the garden.

Harvest Time

Jin and Laurie were excited. It was almost time to harvest the vegetables from their new garden. The late-September weather had just turned cool, and the crops that they had planted in the spring were ripe and ready to be picked.

Laurie stood near the gate of the white wooden garden fence with a yellow bucket in her hand. She was going to collect the plump sweet peppers and skinny hot peppers. The branches of each short pepper bush sagged under the weight of the plentiful and heavy green, yellow, and red fruits. Laurie was anxious to start picking, but she promised Jin that she would wait for him.

Just as Laurie was about to yell for Jin, he emerged from the house wearing dirty gardening gloves and carrying a small saw. He wanted to collect some of the spotted gourds and squashes. The pumpkins on the largest vine had been growing for months and were larger than Jin's head! "Sorry I took so long," Jin said. "I couldn't find my other glove."

"No problem," Laurie said. "I've been looking forward to this. I told you that this soil would produce some great food!" They walked through the gate and stepped carefully around the rows of plants.

"How did you know?" Jin asked.

"I didn't just *know*," said Laurie. "I dug up the dirt and tested it." She picked up a handful of the black earth and brought it close to her nose. "You can smell how rich the soil is."

"Wait until I work my cooking magic on the produce!" Jin said as he began sawing the thick stem of a fat pumpkin. "I promise it'll smell much better than dirt."

SKILL PRACTICE Read the item. Write your response.

1. Where is this garden most likely located? Explain.

_____

_____

2. Why are the children excited?

_____

_____

3. Who probably had the idea to create the garden? How can you tell?

_____

STRATEGY PRACTICE Underline the words or phrases that helped you visualize Jin and Laurie's garden.

WEEK 28 — Theme — DAY 3

READ THE PASSAGE Think about the author's message in this passage about corn.

King Corn

Corn is one of the most important crops in the world. We eat it, we turn it into fuel, and we feed it to pets and farm animals. Corn is even partly responsible for the survival of early settlers in North America. But for all its usefulness, corn—a member of the grass family—was once considered little more than a weed.

Unlike today's corn plants, which produce ears up to a foot (30 cm) long, the ancestor of the modern cornstalk was much smaller. The cobs of the ancient plant were only about two inches (5 cm) long. Native Americans noticed that the tiny, hard corncobs could be boiled or ground and then eaten, so they began working with the crops to try to grow bigger ears of corn. To do this, they selected and replanted seeds from the plants that produced the largest ears. Their hard work paid off, and eventually the plants were producing nutritious, tasty, and plentiful amounts of corn.

Over the next several centuries, people developed thousands of varieties of corn. Only about a hundred varieties exist today, but corn is used in more ways than ever. The majority of American cows, chickens, and pigs eat corn in one form or another. Corn syrup is a popular sweetener used in breads, jellies, candy, and soft drinks. Cornstarch can be used instead of plastic or paper to make containers. Once considered little more than a funny kind of grass, corn has become one of the world's most useful resources.

SKILL PRACTICE Read the item. Write your response.

1. What is the theme of this text?

   _____

   _____

2. What is the main idea of the second paragraph?

   _____

3. Name three details that support the fact that corn is now used in many ways.

   _____

   _____

STRATEGY PRACTICE Explain how the first sentence of paragraph 3 provides a transition between the main idea in the second paragraph and the main idea in the third paragraph.

_____

_____

WEEK 28 — Theme — DAY 4

READ THE PASSAGE Think about the themes in the passage as you read.

Competition on the Dance Floor

Many people enjoy dancing with friends at parties or concerts. Sometimes, though, dancing isn't simply fun—it's a contest! All over the world, dancers compete to prove who is the best.

Ballroom dance is one of the oldest forms of dance competition. Couples compete in different categories according to their level of experience. Each category has its own set of dances. Couples are judged on the beauty, accuracy, and difficulty of their dance routines.

Stage dances—such as ballet, jazz, hip-hop, and tap—also have competitions. In these events, dancers usually compete according to age group. Stage dance has many different styles of music, and the dance steps vary. The competitions usually are judged by professional dancers.

Dance battles are another type of contest. They usually consist of a street-dance style such as break dancing. Dance battles began as informal contests between groups of dancers in different neighborhoods. Although many battles are still informal, others are well-organized contests. Dancers can compete alone or in a group. Dance battles can be decided by a panel of experts or simply by the reaction of the crowd cheering and clapping.

Whether twirling across a stage or backflipping in front of friends in the park, dancers find a way to show one another their best moves.

SKILL PRACTICE Read the item. Write your response.

1. Which sentence in the text summarizes the theme? Use quotation marks.

2. Write two ways in which informal dance battles differ from stage dance competitions.

3. You see three people dancing on a subway platform. What kind of dance are they probably doing? Explain.

STRATEGY PRACTICE Which type of dance contest was easiest for you to visualize? Why?

Character and Setting / Theme — WEEK 28, DAY 5

READ THE PASSAGE Think about character, setting, and theme in the story as you read.

The Playoffs

Aaron and Gia were in the back seat of the car on the way to the league's all-star game. Aaron poked his fingers through the grates on the catcher's mask in his lap. Gia turned a baseball over and over in her hands. Both played in the same league. Aaron caught for the Cuckoos, and Gia pitched for the Hippos. But they were selected to play for the same team in the all-star game.

"Remember," Aaron said, "if I signal *one,* it's a fastball. If I signal *two*—"

"I know the signals!" Gia interrupted. "I knew them last night when you told me, and I knew them this morning when you told me again!" She took a breath and then grinned. "I guess a first trip to the all-stars can make anybody nervous."

"Me? No way," Aaron said. "I just can't believe they're making you the starting pitcher."

"Ha! You just don't want anyone to see you wince when you catch my fastball," she teased.

"I don't want to get too tired chasing down your wild pitches," Aaron replied.

"Enough!" Mom said from the driver's seat. The twins saw her expression in the rearview mirror. Aaron pulled on his catcher's mask to cover his face, and Gia squirmed. "You both worked hard this season," Mom said. "So I know you both understand the value of teamwork."

Everyone was silent for a few minutes before Gia turned to her brother. "You know," she said, "Ronny was the Hippos' best hitter, but he's afraid of fastballs." Then she grinned. "Too bad he's on the other team today," she added.

Aaron's face lit up. "Yeah! Bring on the fastballs, Sis! And Marcus was the Cuckoos' best base stealer, but I could always tell when he was about to steal a base. Too bad he's on the other team today, too," Aaron sneered. "You and I have nothing to worry about."

SKILL PRACTICE Read the item. Write your response.

1. What is the setting of this text?

___

2. Name two adjectives that apply to both siblings. Explain your choices.

___

3. Why are both characters smiling at the end of the story?

___

STRATEGY PRACTICE Explain to a partner why it's important for writers to follow the rule of beginning a new paragraph when the speaker in a story changes. How does it help readers?

Author's Purpose — WEEK 29, DAY 1

READ THE PASSAGE Think about why the author wrote the passage.

The Goldilocks Planet

Almost every astronomer has secretly dreamed of discovering a planet where the conditions for life are like those on Earth. In 2010, astronomers and science fans were thrilled to hear about the possible existence of a planet that is big enough and warm enough to support life.

Scientists are calling the planet *Gliese 581g* (GLEE-zuh 5-81-jee). It appears to be part of a solar system that is 20 light-years away from Earth. That's about 500 million times farther away than the moon is—much too far away for humans or even satellites to visit. Scientists must use special equipment to study such faraway objects in space.

One method that scientists use is to study radio waves. All objects in space emit radio waves, but most of these waves are random signals. They don't have a pattern. Scientists hope to find a pattern in the radio waves coming from Gliese 581g, which might mean that there are life-forms on the planet smart enough to use radio waves the way humans do.

If scientists could study the atmosphere of Gliese 581g, they might find gases and other chemicals that would prove that life-forms existed there. First, though, scientists would have to find the exact location of Gliese 581g. Even then, studying the atmosphere of a planet that is billions of miles away from Earth won't be possible for another few decades.

If Gliese 581g really does exist, the chances are incredibly small that it has intelligent life similar to that on Earth. Even if there were such life on the planet, it's doubtful that you could have a pen pal from Gliese in your lifetime. However, the possibility that we are not alone in the universe has scientists, and many others, looking into space with a new sense of excitement.

SKILL PRACTICE Read the item. Write your response.

1. Why did the author write this text?

2. What is the purpose of the second paragraph?

3. What is the purpose of the last paragraph?

STRATEGY PRACTICE With a partner, think of four questions you would ask scientists who are studying Gliese 581g.

Author's Purpose — WEEK 29, DAY 2

READ THE PASSAGE Think about the author's purpose for writing each section.

The History and Future of Special Effects

Special effects in movies can seemingly make dinosaurs come to life and spaceships soar through the galaxy. Most of today's effects are created with computers. But special effects themselves are not new. Here are some important moments in the history of movie effects.

The Beginning of Movies

When audiences in Paris, France, viewed the first projected movies in 1895, they were stunned. Movies that might seem ordinary to us now were brand-new to viewers. Some early filmmakers, such as Georges Méliès (may-lee-ES), experimented with such film tricks as making objects "disappear" or change size. One of Méliès' movies, *A Trip to the Moon* (1902), was about a spacecraft that lands on the moon and was one of the best special-effects movies of its time.

Models and Miniatures

Before computers, many filmmakers used models of monsters and miniature buildings to create special effects. Both *King Kong* (1933) and *Godzilla* (1954) were made using tiny models to depict an enormous monster. Each model was positioned and photographed carefully to make it seem as if the creature were moving through a real city.

The Future of Special Effects

Many filmmakers use special cameras and other equipment to create movies that people watch in 3-D. Monsters and spaceships seem to leap from the screen, making audiences feel as if they are in the middle of the action. As technology advances, there is no telling what future films will look like. But they are sure to continue thrilling moviegoers.

SKILL PRACTICE Read the item. Write your response.

1. What was the author's purpose for writing this text?

_____

_____

2. Why did the author use headings in the text?

_____

3. Why did the author include the names of some movies?

_____

STRATEGY PRACTICE Describe some special effects that you have seen in a movie or on a TV show.

_____

_____

Prediction — WEEK 29, DAY 3

READ THE LETTER   Use information in Shawna's letter to help you make predictions.

> Dear Dad,
>
> After three days of basketball camp, I am still surviving and I still like basketball. In fact, this has been a really fun week so far!
>
> On Monday, I was placed in a group with eight other kids. We chose our own team name, the "Sharks." We also met our coach, Robin. She used to play basketball for the Women's National Basketball Association! She told us we would be the best team at camp if we practiced hard.
>
> Yesterday we worked on drills. It was boring, and my teammates thought so, too. Coach Robin gave us a talk about how important basics such as dribbling and passing are, but she let us play a pickup game at the end of practice.
>
> Today we're working on our free throws. You can probably guess that I'm super nervous about this. I don't know why I have trouble with free throws, but maybe Coach Robin will show me what I'm doing wrong.
>
> I have to go now. My teammates Ana and Monette are here. I'll see you on Saturday!
>
>   Love,
>   Shawna
>
> (P.S. Thanks for giving me those stamps before you left!)

SKILL PRACTICE   Read the item. Write your response.

1. What is Shawna most likely to do after she writes the letter?

2. What do you predict will happen if Shawna continues to practice her basketball skills?

3. Name three skills that Shawna will want to show her father when she gets home. How do you know?

STRATEGY PRACTICE   What question would you ask Shawna about her basketball camp experience?

Prediction — WEEK 29, DAY 4

READ THE PASSAGE Make predictions as you read this passage about blood donation.

The Gift of Life

Seeing blood in a horror movie might make you scream or cover your eyes, but real blood isn't scary at all. Blood keeps us alive. That's why blood donors are considered lifesavers.

Blood donors are people who give blood—usually about a pint (0.47 L) at a time—to blood banks or blood donation centers. The blood is then available for people who have lost blood in accidents, need surgery, or have a serious illness that requires their blood to be replaced. Hospitals and blood banks store the blood and try to keep enough on hand for major emergencies, such as tornadoes and earthquakes, in which many people are injured.

Donating blood is easy. Medical workers ask donors several questions about their health, as well as test their blood, to make sure the blood is safe to use. Then the donors relax, often reading a magazine or talking as their blood is drawn. Afterward, the donors may receive some juice or water and maybe fruit or cookies to give them energy before leaving the donation center. The whole process is simple and quick, not scary. Most people are able to donate blood again in about two months if they wish.

To give blood, a person must be at least 17 years old and must meet certain other requirements. Students of all ages, though, can learn more about the donation process by visiting a local blood donation center. Donating blood is one of the easiest ways to save lives and help a community.

SKILL PRACTICE Read the item. Write your response.

1. What would most likely happen if a fifth grader tried to donate blood?

2. What is a hospital apt to do immediately after a major natural disaster?

3. What might happen to patients if medical workers did not test donor blood?

STRATEGY PRACTICE Describe another way that people can help their communities besides donating blood.

Author's Purpose
Prediction
WEEK 29 DAY 5

READ THE PASSAGE Think about the author's purpose and make predictions as you read.

The World's Biggest Birthday Cake

You may have seen a big cake at a party, but you've probably never seen anything like the world's biggest birthday cake. This seven-layer cake was made from 30,000 sheet cakes and 40,000 pounds (18,144 kg) of frosting. The entire cake was 102 feet (31 m) long and weighed an incredible 300,000 pounds (136,078 kg)—more than 35 full-grown African elephants!

The creation was designed for the 100th birthday of the city of Las Vegas in 2005. For this special anniversary, the city asked for help from bakeries and volunteers. The cake had to be shipped in pieces before volunteers put it together and frosted it.

Once the cake was completed, the birthday party began. Officials from the Guinness Book of World Records declared that the enormous cake outweighed the previous record holder by 128,360 pounds (58,223 kg). After the cake was judged, city leaders and the crowd admired the massive creation for a short time before digging in with forks and knives. They took huge pieces of the cake away on plates and trays.

The cake fed a warehouse full of volunteers and party guests. People ate as much as they could and gave away as much as possible. But even then, the cake was still mostly intact. Later, workers had to take apart the cake just so they could move it. In the end, this gigantic treat was more like a piece of art than a dessert.

SKILL PRACTICE Read the item. Write your response.

1. What is the purpose of the first paragraph?

___

2. What is the purpose of the last paragraph?

___

3. What probably happened to the cake after the party ended?

___

STRATEGY PRACTICE Write two questions that you would ask about the world's biggest birthday cake.

___

Nonfiction Text Features — WEEK 30, DAY 1

READ THE INFORMATION — Notice the different features of the index and recipe.

INDEX (B–C)

Breads, 55–75
 almond, 70
 cherry, 64–65
 cranberry, 59
 date loaf, 73
 gluten-free, 68
 grain, 55–58
 sourdough, 67
 wheat, 74
 zucchini, 71–72

Cakes, 25–54
 apple, 52
 cheesecake, 27
 chocolate, 50
 fudge center, 49
 lemon, 29
 marzipan, 48
 pumpkin, 43–44
 red velvet, 42
 vanilla, 31–33

Cheesecake, 27

Cherry bread, 64–65

Cherry pie, 98

Chocolate cake, 50

Cookies, 76–92
 bran, 90
 chocolate chip, 76
 drop, 80
 Easter, 88–89
 flour-free, 91
 gingerbread, 82
 peanut butter, 85
 rice, 84
 rosette, 92
 snickerdoodle, 83

Custard, 15–24

Zucchini Bread

This dense bread has the flavors of cinnamon and spice. You won't even taste the zucchini!

Ingredients

 2 cups all-purpose flour
 1 cup wheat flour
 1 teaspoon salt
 1 teaspoon baking soda
 1 teaspoon baking powder
 3 teaspoons ground cinnamon
 3 eggs
 1 cup pureed pumpkin
 1 cup white sugar
 1 cup brown sugar
 3 teaspoons vanilla extract
 3 cups grated zucchini

Directions

1. Grease and flour two 8" x 4" loaf pans. Preheat oven to 325°F.
2. Sift flour, salt, baking soda, baking powder, and cinnamon into a bowl.

SKILL PRACTICE — Read the item. Write your response.

1. Which four ingredients in the zucchini bread are used in equal amounts?

2. What will readers find if they turn to page 83?

3. Why is the recipe for cherry bread included in two locations in this index?

STRATEGY PRACTICE — Name two other topics that might be listed in the index as shown.

Nonfiction Text Features — WEEK 30, DAY 2

READ THE APPLICATION Think about the special features and details given on the application.

Marsh County Fourth of July *Kids & Pets Parade*
APPLICATION FORM

Name: _Rebecca Lee_   Age: _11_   Phone number: _(312) 555-3271_
Participating pet's name: _Snuggles_   Type of pet: _Puppy_
Other materials used: _bicycle, bicycle helmet, sparklers, red wagon_
Description of parade activity: _Rebecca will ride her bicycle along the parade route while wearing a helmet and other safety gear. A red wagon will be attached to the bicycle. Snuggles will ride in the wagon and do tricks for the crowd. Rebecca will safely attach sparklers to her bicycle to fit the Fourth of July theme._

Are you entering the costume contest? Yes ☒   No ☐
Name of costume: _"Dorothy and Toto on the Fourth of July"_

IN CASE OF EMERGENCY
Adult contact name: _Maddie Lee_   Relation to participant: _Grandmother_
Adult contact phone: _(312) 555-3271_
Will the contact person be attending the parade? Yes ☒   No ☐

SKILL PRACTICE Read the item. Write your response.

1. What is the purpose of this form?

2. According to the application, who wants to participate in the Fourth of July parade?

3. Will Rebecca's emergency contact person be at the parade? How do you know?

STRATEGY PRACTICE Why do you think the emergency contact information is in a separate box from the rest of the application?

Visual Information — WEEK 30 DAY 3

READ THE INFORMATION Look carefully at the illustrations of blood cells, and read the captions.

Cells in the Blood

Blood is made of cells floating in a liquid called *plasma*. This liquid brings nutrients to cells and carries away waste. Blood contains three types of cells or cell parts: red blood cells, white blood cells, and platelets.

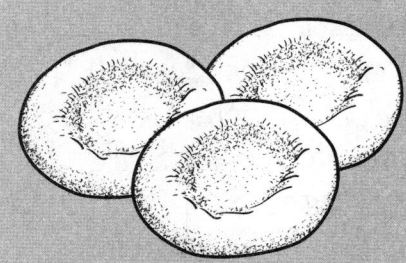

Red blood cells
- Give blood its color
- Make up 99% of all blood cells
- Deliver oxygen to the body

Platelets
- Contain pieces of larger blood cells
- Collect at the site of a cut or scrape to help blood form a scab

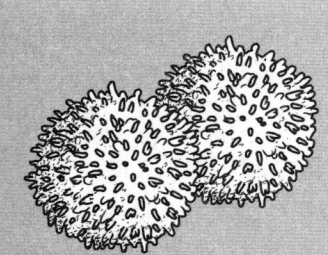

White blood cells
- Fight infection in the body
- Normally are outnumbered by red blood cells

SKILL PRACTICE Read the item. Write your response.

1. Which type of cell is the most plentiful? How can you tell?
   _____
   _____

2. You fall off your skateboard and scrape your knee. Which part of your blood helps form the scab?
   _____
   _____

3. Which part of human blood contains platelets, red blood cells, and white blood cells?
   _____

STRATEGY PRACTICE How would this information help someone who is learning about the role that blood plays in keeping the body working and healthy?
_____
_____

Visual Information

WEEK 30 DAY 4

READ THE INFORMATION Study this image of the former president's car.

The Toughest Car in the World

Each president of the United States is given a special car that is built to meet every need, from protection to communication. Here are a few features of former president Barack Obama's car.

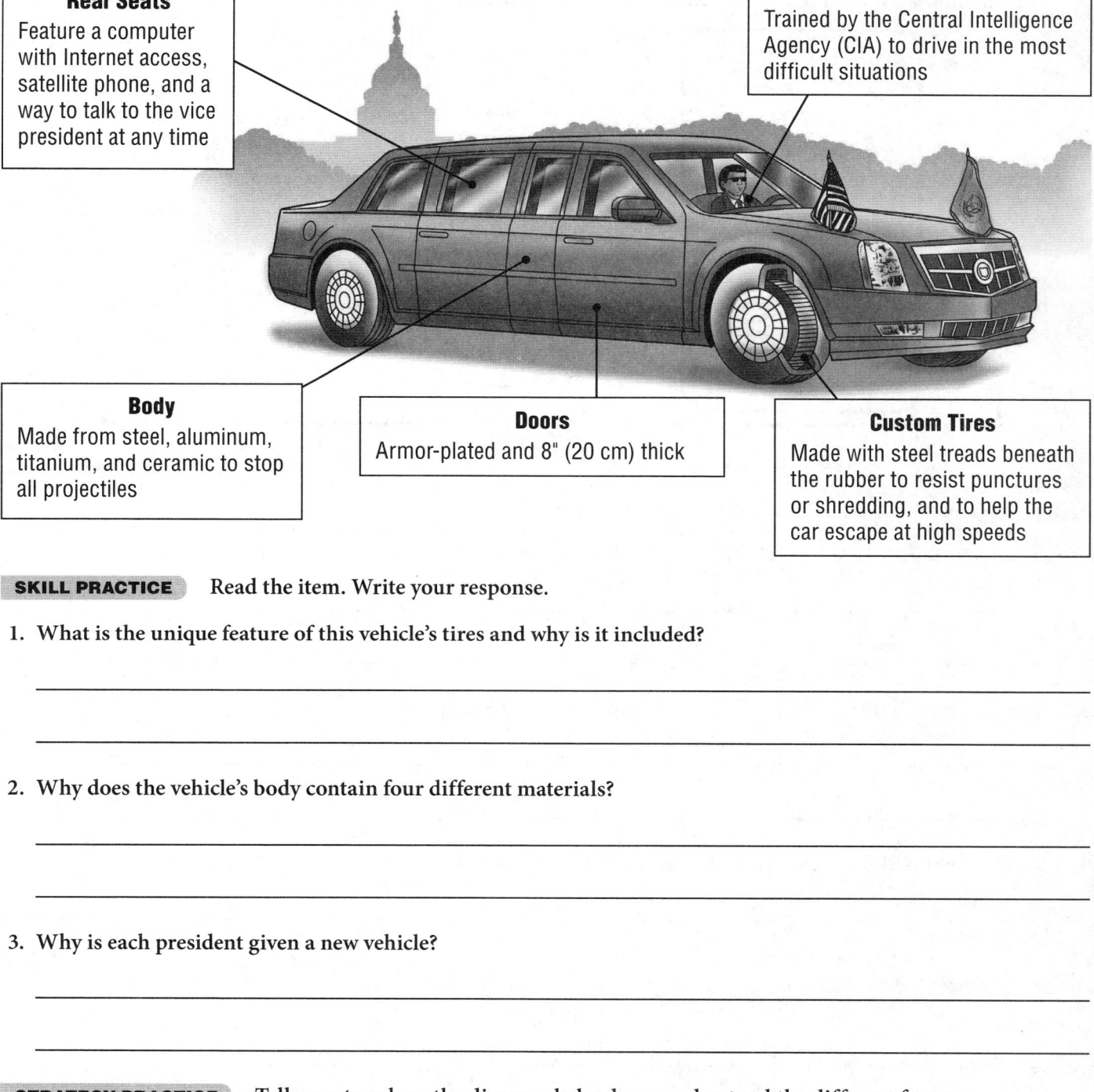

Rear Seats
Feature a computer with Internet access, satellite phone, and a way to talk to the vice president at any time

Driver
Trained by the Central Intelligence Agency (CIA) to drive in the most difficult situations

Body
Made from steel, aluminum, titanium, and ceramic to stop all projectiles

Doors
Armor-plated and 8" (20 cm) thick

Custom Tires
Made with steel treads beneath the rubber to resist punctures or shredding, and to help the car escape at high speeds

SKILL PRACTICE Read the item. Write your response.

1. What is the unique feature of this vehicle's tires and why is it included?

_____

_____

2. Why does the vehicle's body contain four different materials?

_____

_____

3. Why is each president given a new vehicle?

_____

_____

STRATEGY PRACTICE Tell a partner how the diagram helped you understand the different features of the car.

© Evan-Moor Corp. • EMC 6365 • Daily Reading Comprehension

Nonfiction Text Features — **WEEK 30**
Visual Information — **DAY 5**

READ THE DIAGRAM Read the introduction and study the diagram of a food web.

Food Chain or Food Web?

Do you know the difference between a *food chain* and a *food web*? Food chains show how a living thing such as a plant or an animal gets its energy. A food web is made up of multiple food chains and includes many more plants and animals than a food chain includes. This diagram shows a food chain within a food web of the African savanna.

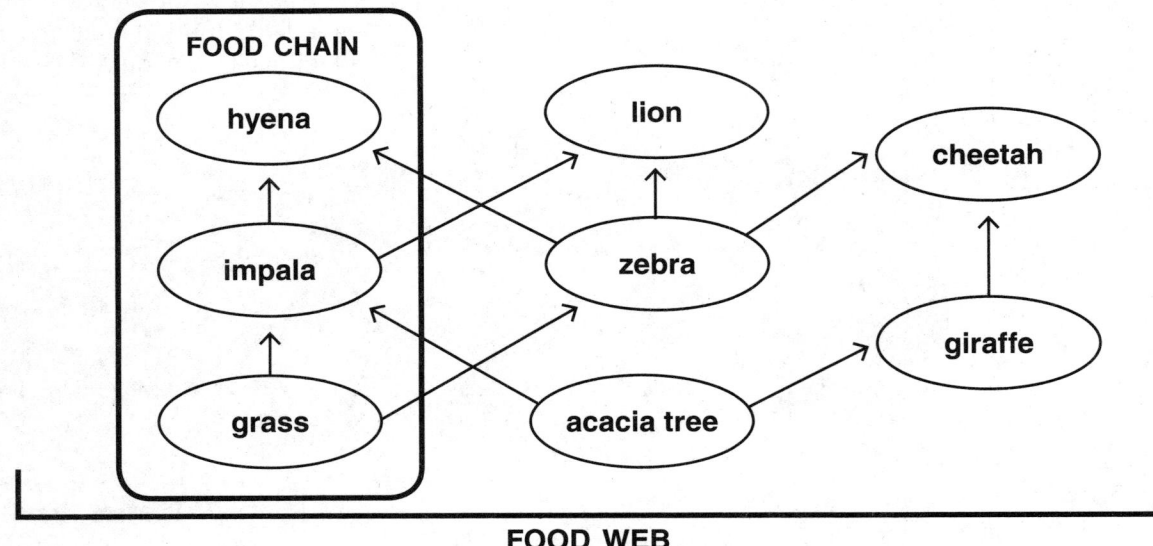

SKILL PRACTICE Read the item. Write your response.

1. Explain why some of the words in the introduction are italicized.

2. Which animals in this food web are eaten by both lions and hyenas? How can you tell?

3. Which animal in this food web eats only acacia trees? How can you tell?

STRATEGY PRACTICE How might the diagram help someone who is planning a visit to Africa and wants to see the animals named in the food web?

How to Be a Good Reader

Ask yourself these questions to help you understand what you read:

Main Idea and Details	What is the story mostly about? What tells me more about the main idea?
Sequence	What happens first, next, and last? What are the steps to do something?
Cause and Effect	What happens? (the effect) Why did it happen? (the cause)
Fact and Opinion	Can this be proved true? Is it what someone thinks or believes?
Compare and Contrast	How are these people or things the same? How are these people or things different?
Make Inferences	What clues does the story give? What do I know already that will help?
Prediction	What clues does the story give? What do I know already that will help? What will happen next?
Character and Setting	Who or what is the story about? Where and when does the story take place?
Theme	What lesson does this story teach? How does the author feel about this topic?
Author's Purpose	Does the story entertain, inform, try to persuade me, or teach me how to do something?
Nonfiction Text Features	What kind of text am I reading? What does it tell me?
Visual Information	Is there a picture, chart, or graph? What does it tell me?

My Notes

My Notes

My Notes

My Notes

My Notes

My Notes